An Imperfect Pilgrim

Trauma and Healing on This Side of the Rainbow

Suzanne Ludlum

BALBOA.
PRESS

A DIVISION OF HAY HOUSE

Balboa Press books may be ordered through booksellers or by contacting:

Balboa Press
A Division of Hay House
1663 Liberty Drive
Bloomington, IN 47403
www.balboapress.com
1 (877) 407-4847

Because of the dynamic nature of the Internet, any web addresses or links contained
in this book may have changed since publication and may no longer be valid. The views
expressed in this work are solely those of the author and do not necessarily reflect the
views of the publisher, and the publisher hereby disclaims any responsibility for them.

The author of this book does not dispense medical advice or prescribe the use of any
technique as a form of treatment for physical, emotional, or medical problems without the
advice of a physician, either directly or indirectly. The intent of the author is only to offer
information of a general nature to help you in your quest for emotional and spiritual well-
being. In the event you use any of the information in this book for yourself, which is your
constitutional right, the author and the publisher assume no responsibility for your actions.

Any people depicted in stock imagery provided by Thinkstock are models,
and such images are being used for illustrative purposes only.
Certain stock imagery © Thinkstock.

Print information available on the last page.

ISBN: 978-1-5043-7824-6 (sc)
ISBN: 978-1-5043-7826-0 (hc)
ISBN: 978-1-5043-7825-3 (e)

Library of Congress Control Number: 2017905208

Balboa Press rev. date: 05/02/2017

For Charlie

The love of my life

You need to take the traumas and make them a part of who you've come to be ... to take the worst events of your life and fold them into a narrative of triumph.

—Andrew Solomon, writer and lecturer

Contents

Acknowledgments

Gratitude is offered to the writers whose permission has allowed me to grace these pages with their words of wisdom: Andrew Solomon, PhD, writer, lecturer, winner of the National Book Award, and mental health activist; Steven Cuoco, best-selling author of *Guided Transformation: Poems, Quotes and Inspiration*; Teal Swan, inspirational speaker; Shannon L. Alder, author of *300 Questions LDS Couples Should Ask Before Marriage*; John Welwood, psychologist and author of *Toward a Psychology of Awakening*; Nancy Slonim Aronie, author of *Writing from the Heart*; Peggy Haymes, author of *Strugglers, Stragglers and Seekers: Daily Devotions for the Rest of Us*. Your words reached deeply into my heart.

To Charlie, my partner, best friend, and biggest fan, for your unwavering love and support; my dear friend Barbara, who believed in me long before I did; Denise, who never left me; and my wider circle of friends who are too many to list—you are also my family. And for my daughters, Leala and Katie, who, aside from this book, are the greatest accomplishments of my life.

From the Author

This book has been in the making for thirty-five years, and during most of that time, the writing occurred in my head. I knew I would write my story one day, but what I couldn't know then was that so much of it had yet to be lived. When I knew it was time to put pen to paper, I was eager and scared at the same time. It's been said that memoir writers live twice. For some of us, the first time was bad enough, so why go there? That was the gnawing question I kept asking myself: Why do it? I knew it had to serve a purpose beyond myself, and so I let go of the question and drew on faith that the answer would reveal itself at the right time.

After some time went by, I began to hear a voice. It started as a whisper in my ear, then a tap on my shoulder. Then it woke me in the night and followed me around during the day. It was saying, "*The time is now.*" I took a closer look and saw the answer materialize: inspire *hope*.

So I got to work. I wrote in coffee shops, in restaurants, in hotel rooms, in an apartment I rented one summer in San Francisco. I wrote at a mountain lake retreat and at my kitchen table, in libraries and waiting rooms and at a picnic table in the woods. I became afraid of what I was seeing on the paper and, as I tend to do, looked for something to take me away from that which made me afraid. So I went to graduate school for two years. After graduation, I found myself filling time with lists of other projects but always hearing that little voice saying, "Uh, ready to get back to that book of yours?"

Then shortly after, my husband and I were in a serious car accident that left me incapacitated for several months. I think that was God's way of telling me that I had no more excuses and plenty of time, so get on with it already.

So here it is. It's true that this is a story of trauma, loss, depression, hopelessness. However, it is also a story of determination, survival, and joy. I'm throwing it out there like a message in a bottle. If my story can touch just one person, keep one person off the ledge, or give hope to someone who has no more left, then my experience was worth it. Every life is sacred, and maybe this book will serve as a conduit to ignite a spark of hope to those who believe they are at the end of their rope. A great motivational speaker is quoted as saying that if a life is worth living, it's worth recording. This is a record of my life.

To all of you who are living in darkness: Hang On, Pain Ends.

I kneel onto my mat, sit back on my heels, and lean forward in supplication with my forehead on the floor. With spring-loaded action, the tears burst forth and spill out. My limp body surrenders to gravity as an oily mixture of tears, snot, and drool collects in a puddle underneath me and the air swallows my cries. My mat is the only familiar thing I know right now. It has borne witness to the entirety of my emotions, from pain and sadness to white-hot anger, to total bliss. It's my friend and companion and accepts me for all the wonderful and terrible things I am.

"Where you been?" my mat asks.

"Sorry, got distracted," I reply in my mind.

"S'okay, welcome back."

My mat doesn't judge me, and it never makes me feel guilty for neglecting it. Each time I step onto it, I feel welcomed as though it's the first time. It doesn't matter what I did yesterday or what I'll do tomorrow; what's important is that I'm here now, whether I cry, breath, move, or sit in stillness and simply Be.

—SL

Prologue

The podium stands tall and proud between the first row of desks and Mr. Christophe's desk in the front of the classroom. The tape recorder rests on the lip of the podium set on "pause." I'm sitting in the second row from the right, third desk from the front, facing the blackboard in seventh grade History class. Today we're presenting our reports on westward movement. We're being recorded so Mr. Christophe can listen to our oratories later while grading the papers. History is a subject that bores me to no end, and I'd rather be anywhere but here right now. My mind drifts out of the classroom, down the hall to the room where Bobby sits.

Bobby is my first crush in middle school and he's absolutely *adorable*. He's thin with small brown eyes and brown wavy hair and has a sort of sexiness that I find very appealing. Maybe he reminds me of my real One True Love whom I fell in love with when *The Partridge Family* first aired on television. David Cassidy had a perfect smile that lit up his perfect eyes, and I loved watching his perfect body rock in rhythm as he played his guitar. I'd make sure I was home every Friday night to watch it, and I never missed an episode. I also made sure to get tickets to every one of his concerts when he came through New Jersey … I'd ride home with my throat on fire, my vocal chords shredded from screaming "DAVID! I LOVE YOU, DAVID! I LOVE YOUUUU!" Since David hasn't noticed me yet but Bobby has, that's where I park my evolving libido. I think Bobby likes me too; at least that's what my girlfriends say. Once he even smiled at me as we passed in the hallway!

My mind is quickly pulled back into the classroom as Mr. Christophe calls my name. I grab my hand-written report and walk to the podium. I've always loved being in the front of the class. In fourth grade, my poster presentation of the hazards of cigarette smoking was so good that my teacher Mr. Baker asked me to present it to all the fourth grade classes. The accolades echoed in my memory for months.

Mr. Christophe had instructed us on how to operate the tape recorder, so I switch the button to the "on" position and begin reading from my paper.

I'm feeling different today. Not my usual relaxed self. I feel my heart begin to pound in my chest, and then it begins to beat faster and faster. It's fluttering, and I'm having a hard time breathing. My throat is tightening, and the air won't go in or out. I feel a burning sensation bursting forth from the center of my chest as a river of heat flows through my body like a flame racing along a fuse. My cheeks are on fire, and I feel beads of sweat forming on my eyelids. My hands begin to shake, and my voice has an unnatural vibrato that I can't control. Stunned, I stop reading and try to catch my breath. I look out at the sea of pubescent faces to see no one moving. Their eyes are wide open, staring at me. I begin again, and again my body breaks into spasms that feel like an epileptic seizure. My legs turn to mush, and I lock my knees so I don't collapse onto the floor. I hear giggling and snickering from my classmates, and this time I don't dare take my eyes off my paper, which becomes a crackling, crinkling pile of pulp in my trembling hands. The ink on the page smears from the sweat on my hands, and it's hard to read the words. When I do look up again, I'm looking through some sort of film that coats my eyes and I can't see. The room is suctioning inward and disappearing into a vortex of terror, and I have no bearing as to where I am in space. I'm reading faster now, just to get it over with. I don't know what's happening to me. Am I having a heart attack? At twelve years old? In history class?

Thank God I finally finish, and with jelly-like legs I make my way back to my seat, feeling the prickly sensation of twenty-three pairs of eyes on me. I want to cry. The back of my neck stiffens, and I feel the exhaustion of a novice marathoner. Now here's where it *really* gets fun. After each student presents, Mr. Christophe plays back the recording for the class to hear. In my mind, I'm begging him to just please skip this one; I don't think I can bear hearing myself fall to pieces in front of everyone. I watch him walk slowly to the front of the room and hit the "play" button, and I sink lower in my seat, my head hanging low. Hey, God, now would be a really good time to open up the earth and let me fall in, thank you very much.

The recording plays and I'm forced to listen. I'm suddenly Alex DeLarge, the character villain in *A Clockwork Orange*, strapped to a chair facing a movie screen with his eyelids held open with small metal clips, squirming as he's forced to watch a scene of unimaginable violence. There's nowhere to hide; there's nowhere to run. I'm trapped. I peek around the room and see everyone—even Mr. Christophe and my friend Debbie—laughing out loud as the shaming sound of my trembling voice plays on. I'm holding my breath and trying hard to lock the tears behind my eyes.

I want to die.

When it's over, I sit frozen in my seat, naked and exposed. No one utters a word for what seems like forever. The humiliation I feel is compounded by the betrayal of my peers. Mr. Christophe eventually calls on the next student while I stare at the surface of my desk. I vow to never be trapped again. I will run. For my life.

The Disembodied Parent

All happy families are alike; each unhappy
family is unhappy in its own way.

—Leo Tolstoy

When I was about three years old, my sister Liz and I discovered that we could sit on the floor in our bedroom closet and tie the dangling ribbons of our dresses together to make a swing for our Barbie dolls. That was our first playroom, until our mother appeared in the doorway and discovered the mess we made of our neatly pressed dresses. Her face wasn't visible from the floor where I sat, only her legs. But her anger hung low in the air and wafted toward me, fueling the tears that fell as she yelled at us to get out of the closet; how dare we taint our pretty clothes. This is one of my earliest memories.

My mother became a woman whose unhappiness poisoned the lives of her children. For reasons unbeknownst to me, she grew to despise my father and made sure my sister and I knew it. When I was around eight, I was given the directive to not love my father anymore. It was revealed to me one evening when Dad came home from work. He had worked late that night, as he did with more frequency; and Mom, my older sister, Liz, and my little brother, Joey, and I were in her bedroom watching television. I heard him come in, and I hopped down the stairs to greet him.

"Daddy's home!" I shouted up to Liz. She didn't come down. I met him at the door and followed him into the living room to the fireplace, where he reached into his pockets and placed keys and coins on the mantle. I looked at him curiously; lately he hadn't shown much enthusiasm toward anything, and I wondered why he was sad. Later that night, Liz whispered to me, "Mommy doesn't want you to love Daddy anymore." I was confused and upset. *Why?* I thought. I didn't understand. This didn't make sense.

With no further explanation, I went on loving him. But I soon began to see that the consequence of doing so was coldness from Mom. If I was nice to him, she was cool to me. The subtle yet visceral vibes I got from her sent a clear message: *it's either him or me.* And not having Mom's love was unimaginable. So I managed, on some level, over time, to convince myself that he really was the malefactor she made him out to be, an outlook that was fueled by stories she shared with Liz and me behind closed doors about the things he supposedly did to hurt her.

Dinnertime was an interesting affair. It became a sitcom, but without the comedy. I'll call it a sitdram, a situation drama. I sat at one end of the table, my sister at the other, Mom and Dad opposite each other on the side, and Joey next to Mom. Dinner usually began in silence. Then someone, usually Mom, made a comment not quite under her breath, and Dad rebutted. The sound of forks against plates, scooping of mashed potatoes out of the bowl, and knives slicing through well-cooked beef served as a curious backdrop to the arguing that oftentimes drew Liz and me into it. The taste of our well-balanced, prepared-from-scratch meal turned sour in my mouth as the fighting escalated.

"You can have your say when you're eighteen," Dad said when one of us spoke up to offer an unsolicited opinion. Of course, Mom felt differently because we usually sided with her. We were well trained that way: maintain your alliance to her and she'd let you say or do anything.

I was insulted at his rebuttal toward me, and, knowing Mom had my back, offered up whatever thoughts an ill-informed adolescent could muster. I felt empowered, never realizing the hurt our one-sided allegiance caused him. Dad had, by then, become a powerless entity in our home. Mom had made it clear long before that she, not he, was our parent, at least in spirit. I didn't know then that he did value our opinions, that his dinnertime mandate was more of an attempt to not draw us into the sparring match between them.

So their mealtime bickering usually turned into a ping-pong match, her throwing jabs across the table at him, and him volleying more back. Sometimes it got so loud that it drowned out the clattering of forks and knives, plates and bowls. No wonder I developed stomach problems. No wonder Liz became anorexic.

The first time I ran—or tried to run—I was nine. It was another typical sitdram at the dinner table, and attacks were flying. I screamed at them both to just stop it already, jumped from my seat, ran upstairs, and threw whatever clothes were within reach into my flowered canvas suitcase. With my hand gripping its handle and my heart gripping my chest, I hurried back to the kitchen and said to Liz, "I'm leaving. Are you coming with me?"

That seemed to give pause to the volley match, and Mom jumped from her seat, took me by the arm, and walked me back to my room, where I cried and cried, telling her how unhappy I was there. I wanted to run, but I stayed because at nine years old I had nowhere to go and certainly no money to take me there. We talked, I cried, and by the end of the night, I lay in my bed, hopeful that my parents' fragmented relationship would find a way to mend itself.

But the next evening came along and with it, the same sitdram only with a different episode. The script had changed, but the message and characters had not. Remarks were muttered, voices had escalated, shouting ensued, and we children of the family became unwilling witnesses, helpless to either stop it or escape.

As the years went by, Dad found reasons to come home later from work. I watched him as he walked upstairs to the bedroom he no longer shared with Mom (she had moved into Liz's room with her). He quietly emptied his pockets, placing the coins in a dish on his dresser. He then neatly folded his handkerchief, removed his suit, and neatly hung it in the closet, taking great care to straighten out the wrinkles and match the creases in his pants. He put on his after-work casual clothes and went downstairs into the kitchen. By then we all would have eaten and cleared out of his way, so he sat by himself at the table and fed in silence on whatever food may have been left in the refrigerator. A reservoir of guilt lay quiet in my gut as I watched my father live in isolation, but by then I was a part of the new family order, and my allegiance was with Team Mom.

Afterward, he'd settle in his brown suede recliner in the corner of the living room and bury his face in a book. It was about this time that Mom's alcohol consumption fueled enough courage to allow her to start making verbal swipes at him. His empty chair at the dinner table meant that she had no target, but now here he was, and she was primed. On good days, he ignored her. Sometimes, though, he would reach his limit and slowly, methodically, release one hand from the book he was holding, raise it in the air, and extend his middle finger in all its glory, his eyes never leaving the page.

On most days, though, his patience wore out and he'd throw a few comments back at her. This volleying would escalate into screaming matches that she again encouraged Liz and me to join in on. Children can't ever be expected to see a situation clearly, and I didn't then. I believed at the time that my behavior was devotion and righteousness toward Mom, but it would be much later before I saw it as blind allegiance out of fear of abandonment on my part and total manipulation and control on my mother's.

I grew up hearing very few stories about my parents' time together before my siblings and I came along. What I do know is that they met while Dad was in graduate school at Cornell University.

Dad grew up in Balboa, Panama, the son of a canal engineer. Although he lived overseas, he was still an American citizen because his mother traveled to her sister's home in Brooklyn to give birth to him, offering her firstborn son the chance to be president of the United States, should he so choose. Two years later, his younger brother, Warren, came along. When Dad was nine, his father died of a heart attack, leaving a young widow with two small boys to raise. She packed up her sons and moved to the States, leaving them in the care of relatives in Bastrop, Louisiana, and headed for New York to learn secretarial skills. Once she was employable, she returned to Bastrop, claimed her boys, and returned to Panama. About five years later, she remarried and soon after gave birth to a baby girl, Mary Lou. The family eventually left Panama and settled near Columbia, South Carolina.

Dad served in World War II as a paratrooper in the Pacific Theatre. Whatever experiences he had there remained far away in Asia because he never spoke of this time in his life. Like a lot of war veterans, he responded to questions with a quiet gaze to the floor and the comment, "It was a long time ago." After the signing of the peace treaty that ended the war, Dad enrolled at Bradley University and earned his degree in business management, then immediately applied to graduate school.

Mom's parents owned a dairy farm with her dad's brothers a few miles outside of town near Ithaca, New York. When the farming business became financially challenging, they sold their interest and bought a large house on Catherine Street, just around the corner from the campus of Cornell. They made extra money renting upstairs rooms to co-eds, and as a graduate student in the university's School of Labor and Industrial Relations, Dad was one of their boarders. Mom was twenty and could easily pass for a young Elizabeth Taylor. At twenty-nine, Dad was tall, blonde, and devilishly good-looking. He had a mischievousness about him that I'm sure Mom found irresistible, and it didn't take long for their whirlwind romance to carry them off to elope. She telephoned her father from Camden, South Carolina, afterward to break the news.

My parents were ecstatically happy at first. That is until ten months after their elopement when the baby Mom delivered died at one day old. Little Mary Pamille was born with birth defects but nothing that couldn't be treated. The story I was told was that she choked on a bottle the nurse left propped in her mouth in the nursery. She was buried in the family cemetery that was along a wide stretch of road outside Batesburg-Leesville, South Carolina. Her grave was next to an oak tree and marked with a small headstone that had a carving of Little Bo Peep next to her name. Mom didn't attend the funeral. Mary Pamille died on October 25. The significance of that date wouldn't be apparent until many years later.

After they lost the baby, Mom and Dad moved in with his parents and Mary Lou. Their house was a large plantation style straight out of *Gone with the Wind*. Noise in the house was kept to a minimum as Mom and Dad were left alone in their sadness. While most of her friends were still in college, she was grieving her dead child.

They moved to New Jersey when Dad was offered a job there. I imagine it was, in part, to leave the sadness behind. They eventually went on to have Liz five years later. Eighteen months after that, I came along, and then Joey five years after that.

My earliest years, between the age of five and eight, were good years. Our family vacations involved hitting the road in our station wagon, pulling our pop-up camper that was tethered to the trailer hitch behind us. Long before the days of mandatory seatbelt use, we'd hang out the opening of our back window and wave to the other cars. Games like "I spy with my little eye" helped those long road trips go faster. Dad's income as an office worker for the New Jersey State Chamber of Commerce didn't allow the luxury of more expensive vacations, but my siblings and I never knew the difference. We grew up camping along the Eastern seaboard, at the Jersey shore, in the Poconos, and in upstate New York. I developed my love of sleeping out in nature during these trips.

Our annual summer visits to Dad's parents' house in South Carolina usually involved spending one night at a Holiday Inn in Virginia. As soon as we arrived at the hotel, Liz, Joey, and I rushed to put on our bathing suits so we could have time in the pool before dinner. In the morning, we shared pancakes and scrambled eggs in the hotel restaurant before loading up in the car again. Driving past the "South of the Border" sign along the highway meant we were only a couple hours away from our grandparents' house, and when I started seeing the beautiful Spanish moss draping the oak trees, I knew we were almost there. Even today, seeing Spanish moss when I travel through the South brings a reminiscent smile.

When we arrived in Walterboro, we tumbled out of the car and into the arms of Grandma Millie and Grandpa Jim. Grandpa Jim had a quiet sophistication about him that was a nice balance to Grandma Millie's chattiness. He seemed ever so tall as I stood next to him and looked up, studying his thick white hair and dark-rimmed eyeglasses. Each visit always included a trip to the local toy store. That was Grandpa Jim's special time with us.

"You kin pick woon thing 'n ahl bah it foe ya," he would say in his unadulterated Southern drawl.

Aunt Lou lived nearby and soon arrived with her four kids. Her two older boys, Walt and Jim, were about the same age as Liz and me. The adults would shoo us outside, so we wandered around the yard, eventually climbing onto a split rail fence, our feet kicking around the fallen needles of the longleaf pines. The yard was full of these majestic trees, and I'd look up, straining to see their tops that often grew over one hundred feet tall, as I breathed in their vague menthol scent. I'd hop off the fence and squat down to pick up a cluster of fallen needles and weave them into a braid or stick figure or some kind of geometric shape, invariably puncturing a fingertip or two with their needle-sharp points. Walt and Jim were true gentlemen, even as children, and that's what made them my favorite cousins. I had never heard anyone say "ma'am" or "sir" before, and my curiosity about them grew in part because their show of respect was in stark contrast to anything I ever saw at home.

Sue, Joey, and Liz 1965

We also took semiannual journeys to Grammy's house in Ithaca, which were just as much fun. We made the five-hour drive in the summer and again at Thanksgiving, driving through the Delaware Water Gap, north into Pennsylvania, and crossing over into New York State. Ithaca sat at the southern tip of Cayuga Lake, one of the long and narrow bodies of water that make up the Finger Lakes region. The landscape was quite dramatic, with hills, steep ravines, waterfalls, and gorges that created the beauty of the town. The house Grammy and Grandpa Harvey built in their later years while he was still alive sat atop a tall hill on the west side of town. My excitement always grew when we had driven through town and crossed a small canal that fed into Cayuga Lake at the bottom of the hill that led to her house. Route 79 was a two-lane road, and it wound up, up, upward, making me feel like we were driving into the clouds. We turned left onto Westhaven Road and drove another half mile or so before reaching Grammy's gravel driveway and her one-story pink house, proudly perched on the hillside overlooking the city of Ithaca.

A large porch extended off the back of the house and provided an expansive view of Cayuga Lake, Cornell University, Ithaca College, and Buttermilk Falls. At night, I'd stand on the porch and hold a pair of heavy binoculars up to my eyes, scanning the distant lights, having fun identifying the landmarks that had become so familiar.

Two girls about the same age as Liz and me lived next door, and the four of us spent most of our time together. Susie and Karen were country girls, with dirty clothes and legs that seemed to have an endless amount of bruises, but that didn't matter to me because, like me, they loved spending all their time outside. A well-used swing was suspended from a tall tree in their backyard. Two long ropes hung from a high branch and were tied to a worn piece of wood at the bottom. Susie and I took turns pushing each other, and I always asked her to push me harder until I could jump off in mid-swing with the exhilarating feeling of flying through the air. Other times, we'd be gone for hours, exploring the fields across the road. It was there during those glorious summer days where I learned how to extract the juice of a honeysuckle flower. In the evenings after dinner, Mom stayed back at the house with Grammy while Dad drove us to Stewart Park on the edge of the lake. There we'd get ice cream cones and ride the carousel as the evening sun cast long shadows over the lake. It surely didn't get better than that.

When our cousins came to our house to visit, Dad dragged the pop-up trailer into the backyard and raised the roof on it so we'd have a place to hang out. When we weren't building forts in the woods on the other side of the river behind our house, we were swimming in the water, jumping off rocks, and seeing who among us could beat the current. We spent weekends and summers floating on inner tubes a half mile downstream, only to carry the tubes back upstream to do it again.

And most nights were family nights. After Liz and I cleared the dishes from the table, Mom and Dad brought out the Monopoly board. We played until every property was purchased, sold, or traded, and one of us would be declared land baron. It's where I learned that a hotel on Park Place was way more valuable than owning Reading Railroad, and you always want to own Boardwalk because it commands the highest rent. Mom taught us card games like Solitaire and Concentration, and sometimes we moved into to the living room for sing-a-longs, learning songs Mom knew from when she was a girl scout. I can still sing the entire rendition of "Eddie Cucha Catcha Cama Tosta Nana Tosta Noka Samma Camma Wacky Brown" from start to finish.

When I was little, Dad's lighthearted outward demeanor made me feel safe. He eagerly went along with silly things, like when I wanted to be referred to by my middle name, Marie (he was the only one in the family who went along with this). On weekends, he ran in circles around the yard, pushing a wheelbarrow with me bouncing around in it, holding onto the sides, laughing with delight. He also instilled in me a belief that I could do anything. My fifty-cent weekly allowance didn't go far, and I wanted to earn more money, so he taught me how to operate our push lawn mower. He demonstrated how to adjust the push-bar, how to fill the gas tank, how to yank on the pull cord, and of course, the proper footwear.

"You always want to wear sneakers," he said. "Safety comes first."

I loved sneaking up on him, and when I jumped out in front of him and shouted "*Ha!*" he laughed and said, "You're as quiet as an Indian! I never heard you coming!" (I'm sure he did). He didn't judge people; he accepted them. When my sister and I wanted to start making our own decisions, his only advice, said with a smile, was, "Use your best judgment, girls." Sometimes I did, oftentimes I didn't. But looking back, I realize that he must have at least hoped we would, and allowing us room to fail was the best way for us to learn.

But somewhere during those years, something changed. By the time I was ten or eleven years old, family nights all but disappeared. Dust gathered on the Monopoly game that now sat on the shelf in the downstairs playroom. The sound of us singing in the evenings was replaced by the squawk of the television. Mom and Dad stopped entertaining, stopped laughing, and stopped sleeping together. An invisible cloud of tension rose in the house. But more visible was the pain reflected in Mom's tears that fell each night as she sat in her bedroom, Liz and I wrapping our arms around her. We said nothing because we just didn't understand. We didn't know why she was crying, or what happened to cause such sadness. We hurt because she hurt.

One thing I knew was that Mom was drinking more. What I didn't know was if her drinking was the cause or result of the wedge that was pushing her and Dad apart. Liz and I didn't notice at first because she turned the spotlight off of herself and onto Dad. He drank too, but he was a quiet drunk, and she was a loud one. She usually fired the first verbal assault that led to their nightly arguments, which often included her publicly chastising him for his drinking.

"Look at him," she'd spew. "He's drunk again."

His only response was "Have another drink, Jan."

And then one day, just like that, he quit. No beer, no hard liquor. He became sober, he started running, and he lost thirty pounds. And while Dad was becoming healthy, Mom's drinking was becoming more obvious, usually revealing itself through her forked tongue. I began to see that her alcohol consumption and her unhappiness were the real sources of the arguments, accusations, and allegations that flew most nights. She used her well-stocked arsenal of insults and accusations to paint a picture of his apparent shortcomings as a husband.

My mother's pain—whatever the cause—fueled her hatred of my father. I'll never know what happened between them to cause the breakdown of their marriage, but she must have felt trapped. I grew up in a time when most people stayed married and most women stayed home, and I'm sure her options seemed limited at best. Perhaps she felt backed into a corner and her only way to fight back was through manipulating her children.

So, over time, my father became a powerless presence in our house. His word was worthless, his authority nonexistent. He kept quiet. His birthdays were all but ignored. I wanted to openly love him as any child naturally would, but the price was too high to pay. Besides, Mom's regular score-keeping of his apparent infractions against her—reporting them to Liz and me—made it easy to convince myself that I shouldn't. Dad never spoke up, never said what she was doing was wrong. I regarded his silence as an unspoken admission of guilt.

Each year, Dad's company had an annual family event called the "float-down," when employees and their families canoed down the Delaware River. Everyone in the office met for sunrise breakfast at a predetermined mountain restaurant near the Delaware Water Gap, followed by climbing into our canoes and spending the day on the water. Dad always rented a rowboat because Liz and I were small, and he would say, "It's safer for you girls." Sometime around midday, we went ashore, unpacked our picnic lunches and enjoyed them under the shade of trees. Then we re-launched for the rest of the ride downstream. This was always a highlight of my summer.

After my parents' marriage began to deteriorate, Dad still made sure we went on our float-down, but the mood in the air had shifted. For a few years, Liz and I were still young enough that we didn't notice. But one year, on the night before we went, Mom brought us into her bedroom, closed the door, and gave us each twenty-five-cent coins to hide in our shoes.

"I'm so afraid he's going to kidnap you. If you can get away, find a phone and call me."

That year's adventure down the river was weighed down with fear and mistrust, and the fun had all but disappeared. As Joey became old enough to go, Dad took him along, but after that year, Liz and I never went again.

When I was fifteen, there was a particularly bad incident. It was Christmas Eve, and the fighting was well underway. I felt immune from punishment, so I mouthed off to Dad. The anger escalated as the words between us became more heated, and then

Mom stepped in. I don't know who threw the first punch, but it eventually led to the two of them in a brawl on the floor. She tried to push him away with her foot, and he grabbed it and twisted. A loud *crack!* caused the commotion to stop, sending Joey, who was nine at the time, running upstairs to call the police.

Imagine the disconnect of this scene: Santa is making his rounds on the fire truck out on the street in front of our house, the neighborhood children lining up to see him, when a police cruiser pushes its way past them, lights and siren blaring. They park in front of our house, and two officers open the door and walk into our living room. Dad sees them, climbs off of Mom, and is escorted into the kitchen by one officer while the other stays in the living room with Mom, who by now is crying. Liz and I huddle around her, and in my mind, I'm trying to reconcile what just happened. Once Mom made it clear she didn't want to press charges, there was nothing more the officers could do. They left, and we divided. Women in one part of the house, men somewhere else. Christmas morning that year was the chilliest in memory.

My parents' drama took up most of their energy and left little remaining for us. Since there wasn't much for me at home, I began looking for attention elsewhere. I sought it from other kids who came from broken homes. Kids who had plenty of liquor in their houses (with easy access that soon landed me in the hospital from alcohol poisoning when I was fourteen), as well as from adolescent neighborhood boys with their own developing libidos.

My first semiserious relationship was with a boy two years older than me who went to a nearby high school. Bruce lived with his dad in a run-down bungalow in the woods and had a car, so it was easy to take off whenever we wanted. I was fifteen, and we were dating for a couple of months when Bruce started showing interest in more of a physical relationship. I didn't share the same feelings he had for me, but I didn't want him to go away either because I liked the attention he gave me. So I let him talk me into doing things I really wasn't comfortable with.

One weekend, his mom invited us both on a camping trip. Bruce and I were alone in her pop-up trailer when he said, "I want you to do something for me."

"What?" I asked.

"I want you to stroke me."

"Uh, okay."

He unzipped his shorts and pulled out his penis and held it in the air so I could get a good look at it.

"Hold it like a broomstick and rub it up and down," he whispered so as not to wake his little brother, who was sleeping six feet away.

I folded my fingers lightly around it and slowly slid my hand up and down.

"No, like this," he said, and wrapped his hand around mine, gripping tightly as he guided my hand. At first, it was squishy like a water balloon, and I thought he was going to squeeze the life out of it. Then it started to feel harder, and I saw Bruce let go, prop himself on his elbows, and drop his head back. The action came to an abrupt halt when we heard his mother's footsteps nearby, and I quickly scurried to the other side of the camper and slid into my sleeping bag, relieved for the interruption.

A few weeks later, Bruce told me he wanted to "go all the way." My curiosity about the actual act was enough for me to agree to it. I'd finally know what it was that my mother never wanted to explain to me.

Bruce picked me up at my bus stop one morning, and we drove to his house after his father had left for work. I was very uncomfortable with the whole idea but didn't object for fear of creating conflict. That, and my growing curiosity about sex, was enough to give it a try. I'd like to smack the person who invented the notion of "the first time" as being all love songs and butterflies because it was anything but romantic. More like awkward, uncomfortable, and messy (and not the least bit pleasurable). I couldn't wait to go home. After that, I decided that even though Bruce said he loved me, sex with him was overrated, and I just couldn't see myself continuing in a relationship that was one-sided. I broke up with him soon after.

As I got a little older and found reasons to stay away from my house, I began to see my father in a different light. He was not the villain Mom made him out to be, but rather, he was a proud man who refused to play her game. I often wondered why he never spoke up. He stood silent while she built her alliance against him with us, the women of the family. I had been so caught up in my own drama, my own need to find ways to cope, that I wasn't aware of the effects the family dynamic was having on my siblings. Liz was in her own world, buried in her books, and losing weight rapidly. Joey was still a young boy who happened to be collateral burden in my mother's eyes. He was his father's son, and therefore just as unwelcome in her life. She ignored him most of the time.

But I could now see my father as a good soul and knew I needed to mend our relationship. Sitting in his car with him one afternoon in a parking lot downtown, out of the blue I said, "I love you, Dad." It was the most natural thing, and the words came from deep within my heart.

"I knew you would say it one day, Sue. I love you too."

And that was it.

The chains that had been locked around my heart for years freely fell, and it was liberating.

When I was much younger, my dad was my hero and taught me to have good judgment. Not by what he said, but by how he lived.

If another driver cut him off, he'd say in a friendly tone, "I guess he really needs to get somewhere. I'd better let him get there!" He was an observer of people, watching without commenting. He let people be themselves and never cast judgment on anyone.

He must have held out hope that the good judgment he tried to instill in me would one day resurface and we could rekindle the father-daughter relationship we had long ago. That day in the car, for me, it did.

Early Teaching

Don't look at it as the long road ahead …
Look at it as one step closer to your destiny.

—Author unknown

When I was sixteen, I received formal training in Transcendental Meditation. I cleaned the house of a husband and wife who were long-time practitioners, and they always asked me to do the bedroom first so they could go in and meditate while I finished the rest of the house. I had never heard this curious word, "meditation," and was intrigued as to what it involved. In my naive teenage mind, I imagined they were suspending themselves upside down from the ceiling, naked, chanting and humming some sacred pagan hymns. Then I imagined them performing sordid sexual acts on each other as some sort of purification ceremony (why did my imagination always involve sex?).

One day I got up the courage to ask the wife what it meant to meditate. She enthusiastically ran to a cupboard and took out several pamphlets to show me.

"It's called Transcendental Meditation. You sit twice a day, repeating a mantra. It's to quiet your mind and bring you peace."

I suddenly felt embarrassed about what I had imagined it was.

She continued, "There's a TM center in Morristown, and they hold introductory meetings once a month. You're welcome to attend, and it doesn't cost anything."

Sex acts notwithstanding, I was still curious so I told Gary, my boyfriend at the time, about it and asked if he could drive us there.

We pulled into a small parking area behind a large house one block from the main square downtown. It was an old colonial that had been purchased by the TM organization and was used for meetings and trainings. As Gary and I sat through the introductory lecture, my interest grew at about the same pace as Gary's waned. At one point, I looked over at him, and he was slumped back in his chair, staring at the ceiling. For the next meeting, I asked my friend Marty if he was interested in going. He also had a driver's license and a car and was more intrigued than Gary about this strange practice.

After completing several required meetings for those who wanted to learn the process, I was told that my time had come to be initiated. I was instructed to bring, among other things, flowers and fresh fruit as an offering to Maharishi Mahesh Yogi, TM's founder and guru. I arrived on the designated evening with the flowers and fruit, and a young man who was to be my host led me to a room on the second floor and closed the door. He knelt down in front of a large picture of the Maharishi and instructed me to do the same. He then told me to place my offering in a dish in front of the picture while he recited some sort of chant or prayer. He kept his eyes closed, and I quietly glanced around the room, feeling a little self-conscious as the eyes of Maharishi stared down at me. Next, my host leaned toward me, cupped his hand over my ear, and whispered a sound I had never heard before into my ear.

"This is your mantram," he said. "It has been specifically chosen for you and should never be spoken out loud or shared with anyone."

He then led me to a large chair and invited me to sit. He said, "You will now have twenty minutes for your meditation. Use your mantram, but remember: don't utter it out loud. Repeat it only in your mind."

Then he left the room.

So there I sat, obediently repeating my mantram. After a couple of minutes, I began to fidget. How am I ever going to last twenty minutes, I thought? I was a runner, and my body was oftentimes in motion; not to mention all the worries and anxieties that constantly took up real estate in my mind. I forgot to ask my meditation host if I was allowed to move.

After what seemed like twenty hours instead of twenty minutes, my host entered the room, sat down in the chair facing me, and asked me how I thought it went and how I felt.

"Err, okay I guess."

The truth was, I felt awful. My body hurt, and I wanted to jump out of my skin. But I had already paid for the training and wanted to give it a chance, so I went home that night promising to devote twenty minutes of my day twice a day to meditating. Besides, one of the benefits my trainers claimed this practice could bring was it would calm my nerves. I was still struggling with panic attacks and running from the fear of having another one. They were happening more often, and I was afraid I'd soon be one of those people who stayed locked in their house, too afraid to ever go out.

So I followed the instructions given to me by my host that evening: I carved out twenty minutes before school in the morning and twenty minutes in the afternoon, sitting on my bed, legs crossed, eyes closed, and I meditated.

Open Road

Life is either a daring adventure, or nothing.

—Helen Keller

My heart shattered the summer before my senior year in high school. To me, the world was ending. Paul was four years older than me but mature beyond his years, or so I thought at the time. At seventeen, I didn't have a good reference point from which to judge other's maturity level, and when I fell in love with him, I fell hard and fast. I even considered quitting school so I could be with him more (he talked me out of it). We were only a few weeks into our romance when he decided I wasn't the right girlfriend. Or he didn't want to be in a relationship. Or my level of maturity was too far below his. Whatever the reason, he dumped me. Hard. I was devastated. I couldn't eat. I couldn't breathe. My mom was worried. I had to do something to get away from the pain, so I did the only thing I knew how to do: I ran. My friend Ben asked if I wanted to join him on a cross-country hitchhiking journey and, always one for adventure, I gladly said yes.

The problem was how to tell my mother. I was seventeen and, legally, she probably could have stopped me, but she knew that I was headstrong and stubborn and ultimately did whatever I wanted to do anyway. I had long lost respect for her as an authority figure and was planning to go no matter what she had to say about it. But I wanted to ease her into the idea first.

I sat down at the kitchen table one afternoon with her. "Ben and I are thinking of going out to Ohio."

"How are you planning to get there?" she asked.

"Uh, we're gonna hitchhike."

Silence.

"Really?" she eventually asked. "And how smart do you think *that* is?"

"We'll be fine," I said. I wasn't afraid because I had no fear.

We argued back and forth a while longer and, realizing she wasn't going to win this one, she finally said, "Don't expect a nice welcome home when you get back."

When I told Dad, the only thing he said was, "Use your best judgment, Sue."

One week later, Ben and I left.

We began our sojourn at the Delaware Water Gap, heading west on Route 80. We stuffed our backpacks with sleeping bags and only the most essential camping supplies, and my best friend, Denise, and Ben's friend Steve dropped us off just over the state line. When they pulled back onto the road, they looked in the mirror and saw that we were already gone. Getting rides wasn't going to be a problem on this trip. I had pulled my long hair into a boy's cap and wore masculine, loose-fitting clothes to disguise myself as a male. At least that's how I appeared from a distance. We simply looked like a couple of young dudes on an adventure.

Our first night was spent in the Mohican State Forest in Ohio. We camped in our pup tent at the top of a ridge that night and made fire bread for dinner.

"Watch this," Ben said.

He took out a small bowl from his pack and poured the right mixture of flour, water, and sugar into it, then stirred it with a branch he had whittled into a thin stirring stick. When the consistency of the mixture became like raw dough, he began pulling it out of the bowl and twisting it around another whittled branch. He then started a fire, held the dough over the open flame, and we took turns rotating the branch so it cooked evenly on all sides. When it looked cooked enough to eat, we pulled pieces off and stuffed them into our mouths. It tasted delicious.

This was only the first night, and I was already forgetting about the pieces of my heart I left on my tear-soaked pillow back home.

The next morning I awoke and, still laying in my sleeping bag, peeked out the opening of our tent. Seeing the glistening of the morning sun contrasting against the long shadows of the trees reminded me of my childhood family camping trips. It was a comforting familiarity that I welcomed. We hiked down the steep embankment that led to the Clear Fork–Mohican River, where I stripped down and waded into the river. I used the bar of soap we brought to wash the bugs and dirt off my skin. The freedom I felt at that moment could be compared to no other time in my life. I was living in the moment, standing in the river, breathing in the warm air, and feeling the cold current flow between my legs. There was no place in the world I had to be except right there.

We decided later that morning that we needed more food supplies if we were going to be camping, so we bought canned goods, fruit, bread, and jam at the general store near the entrance to the state park. Back out on the road, we were picked up right away by a man who happened to have very little to say. When he dropped us off a couple of hours later, I slid out of the backseat first, reached in, and pulled out my backpack. Ben followed behind me. After he pulled his backpack out, he reached in again to grab our bag of food, but before he could get it, the driver sped away. We stood watching in disbelief as the car disappeared with our next several days' worth of food in it.

Our next ride was with two men who were spending the summer traveling the country and living in communes. Their camping gear was on the floor of the backseat, so they moved it to the trunk to make room for us and our packs. We hadn't driven for long when I felt something on my eyebrow. I reached up to pull it off; it was a tick that had already embedded itself on my eyelid. I felt another on my leg and another inside my pants. I looked at Ben, and he was covered with them as well. We yelled to the driver, who pulled the car off to the side of the road just in time for me to open the door and spill out onto the ground.

"No thanks," I said. We reached into the car, yanked out our packs, shook them out, and starting walking, pulling the fangs of those tiny arachnids out of our skin.

Somewhere in Indiana, we caught a ride in a semitrailer whose driver was apparently looking for company. Ben rode shotgun while I spread out in the sleeping quarters behind the seats. The driver didn't talk much, so we stayed quiet as well. He was going south, not west, but it didn't matter to us. We were on the open road, and I figured all roads lead to everywhere eventually. Somewhere between Terre Haute, Indiana, and Marion, Illinois, the driver pulled his rig into a truck stop for the night, and the three of us slept in the same spots we had been sitting. The driver stretched his legs out onto the steering wheel, pulled his hat over his eyes, crossed his ankles and arms, and fell asleep. Ben did pretty much the same. I spread out on the bed behind the seat and was probably the only one of us who had a comfortable sleep that night. In the morning, we drank some of the driver's payload—chilled orange juice.

Later that day we arrived in Memphis. We were about as far south as we wanted to go and asked the driver to let us out. Just before we crossed Interstate 40, Ben and I climbed down out of the truck's cab and threw our backpacks on. We waved good-bye as we watched the rig slowly accelerate with great effort back onto Route 55, the driver toggling through all eighteen gears to get the massive rig back up to travel speed.

Memphis in July is an inferno. The air is so thick you can scoop it up with a bucket. As I stood in the blazing sun on the side of the freeway, one hand extended with my thumb in the air and the other wiping the sweat off my brow, I tried to breathe, but the wet-hot thickness of the air made inhaling difficult. We walked with our thumbs out and eventually found some amount of relief in the shade of an overpass. Also resting there was a man of about twenty-five who had clearly been on the road for some time. His clothes were well worn, and his hair was dirty, long, and unkempt. His name was Marty, and he was on his way to Los Angeles. Marty had been traveling alone since starting out from his Lower East Side apartment in Manhattan and was glad to have traveling companions.

After a while, a white sedan pulled over to the side of the road and an arm extended out from the passenger window, motioning for us to get in. Marty, Ben, and I ran up to the car and looked inside to check out the situation. There must have been five people in the car already, and no one was over the age of seventeen. Not wanting to stay in the heat any longer, we stuffed our backpacks into the trunk beside the two cases of Budweiser and squeezed into the backseat. These kids were serious about having a good time. We listened to dust and gravel fly behind us as the driver jammed his right foot onto the accelerator. After we crossed into Arkansas on Interstate 40, the car picked up even more speed. I watched the odometer climb to 90, 100, 110, and finally peak at 120 miles an hour when I heard an explosion under the hood. The kids were laughing, screaming, and climbing over each other and didn't seem to notice the black smoke pouring out from under the hood until the car decelerated into a slow roll onto the side of the freeway, coming to an involuntary stop, Ben, Marty, and I exchanged a nonverbal signal that it was time to move on. We grabbed our things and started walking, and about a quarter mile down the road, we looked back to see red and blue flashing lights pulled up behind the sedan, which by now had its trunk open. Since I was still underage, I was glad to not be a part of that party anymore.

We walked and walked and walked some more, with no sign of a ride in sight. When darkness fell and, along with it, the hope of covering more roadway, we climbed over the guardrail and into the brush about sixty feet from the highway, rolled out our sleeping bags, and spent the night under the stars.

I had kept up my male disguise for most of the journey, but by then we were so desperate for a ride that I took off my cap, let my hair down, and removed my large flannel shirt, clearly revealing my obvious feminine body. We came up with a plan: Ben and Marty hid in the brush while I stood, thumb extended, wearing my tight jeans and tank top. It worked, sort of. Plenty of cars stopped but then drove away when they saw the two boys appear from out of the bushes. A pickup truck stopped, and I ran up to the driver's side. A man around the age of forty sat looking at me with one arm resting on the steering wheel and the other propped on the door armrest, his chin resting on his hand. His expression was more of a question as he looked at me for a minute without saying anything. He glanced in his mirror to see Ben and Marty run out onto the pavement, and he looked at me with an expression that said, *really?*

"Can my friends come too?" I said with a smile.

He let out a sigh, gazed out into the distance in front of him, and said, "Yeeeaahhhh, get in." I slid into the passenger seat in front while Ben and Marty climbed into the truck bed behind us.

His name was Ron, and he was a professional racecar driver. He was going as far as Phoenix, and I said that was okay with us.

By now, Ben had called his friend in Tucson and asked if we could stay with him for a while before deciding where we'd go next, so that became our destination. Marty would have to finish his trip to Los Angeles without us.

It was late in the day as we drove across the Texas Panhandle. The limitless view of the prairie redefined my idea of "the open road." Rolling plains intermingled with the high plains, and I watched the earth-tone land with its thick grasses, occasional rock mounds, and solitary windmills proudly perched in the distance pass by. I'd never seen such vastness as this, where the endless sky provided a 360-degree view of the endless landscape. Having grown up in a suburban neighborhood just a few miles from New York City in a state where the drive between Pennsylvania and Manhattan was a mere ninety minutes long, my view from the pickup truck left me speechless.

Ron said he knew of a great steak house (where isn't there a great steak house in Texas?), so we stopped in Amarillo. Every table hosted men who had clearly arrived with big appetites. Most of them wore leather and suede hats and boots that were sculpted with stones and leather stitching snaked in various patterns. And, yes, some even had spurs that extended behind and just above their heels. I'd never seen real cowboys before, and it was exciting to be a part of the real Texan scene. And the steaks were *huge*.

Ron decided he wanted to drive all the way through, so that meant spending the night in the truck. Marty was now in the cab with Ron, and Ben and I were in the truck bed. We rolled out our sleeping bags, pulled one into the other like a glove, and both of us shimmied inside, huddling close together to stay warm. I had the naive impression that New Mexico was warm twenty-four hours a day in the summer, and nothing prepared me for the bitter cold we endured that night. To paraphrase a line often attributed to Mark Twain, the coldest winter I ever spent was a summer night in the back of a pickup truck speeding through New Mexico. My long hair whipped wildly in the wind, slapping against my face, and the ice-cold air burned the inside of my nasal passages. We slept very little that night. Sometime in the night, Ben yelled for me to sit up and, looking out into the distance, down into an expansive valley, I saw a breathtakingly beautiful interminable sea of lights that was the city of Albuquerque. I burned the image into my memory.

The next day, it was my turn to sit in the air-conditioned cab up front. Ron and I got to talking and, at one point, he looked at me and said, "Just for the record, how old *are* you?"

"Seventeen!" I said with naive enthusiasm.

He looked away and muttered, "Damn!" Then he turned to me and said, "Young lady, do you have any idea how much trouble I could get into? And do you know what could have happened to you when you ran up to my truck? Dang, if I had been a lesser man ..."

He was right, I was taking careless chances. That moment was the first time I considered that what we were doing was risky in any way.

Along with never having hitchhiked before and not bothering to consider the dangers, and when or if I would ever go home, my underage status and the risks Ben and I were taking was something that never occurred to me. I shook off the uncomfortable feeling and told myself it didn't matter. I was on an adventure.

I turned to Ron and said, "My parents know where I am," (a half truth) "and Ben's eighteen" (a whole truth). We sat without talking a while longer before Ron changed topics.

"You know, I could get you a job at Big Boy's restaurant in Flagstaff. You could wait tables and make some money. I might even be able to find you a little apartment."

I thought about it for a minute, tempted by the thought of life on the road. It certainly appealed to my sense of adventure and held a promise of not having to go home again. But having the offer come from a much older man I hardly knew kinda creeped me out.

"Thanks, but I have to finish school. I'll be a senior this year and probably really should graduate."

"Okay, well, let me know if you change your mind, little lady."

I sat in uncomfortable silence for the next hour, wondering if he was putting the make on me. I liked older men, but he was a little *too* old for me.

Sometime after we crossed the state line into Arizona, I needed to pee, badly. Ron stopped on the side of the road, and I barely made it out of the truck and down an embankment before pulling my shorts down and squatting squarely onto the extended needles of a prickly pear cactus. I let out a yell as the warm yellow stream flowed out of me, watering the cactus underneath. I half-stood, leaning over and hurriedly pulled my shorts back on before any of the three men in my group saw me.

We arrived in Phoenix later that day. Ron pulled off the freeway and onto a side road downtown. We unloaded our gear off the truck, said good-bye to Ron (thankfully), and regrouped under an overpass. It was time for Marty to continue on to Los Angeles, and we were almost to Tucson, so the three of us said our good-byes. We exchanged phone numbers and promised to get together once we were all back home. Then Ben and I found our way to Route 10, extended our thumbs, and headed south to Tucson with a family who picked us up right away.

Ben's friend Rob lived in a clean suburban neighborhood on the edge of town with his parents. Rob was an only child and clearly the product of heavy mothering. His parents were fundamentalist Christians whose strict adherence to Bible teachings left little room for dealing with real-life situations, such as two scraggly wayward teenagers from New Jersey showing up at their door.

"You can sleep here, but your friend will be sleeping at a neighbor's house down the street, praise the Lord," she told Ben that evening.

I'd have none of that and told Ben as much. "Hey, we just traveled across the entire country together, and I'm not about to be sent down the street to a stranger's house," I told him in frustration.

He pleaded our case to Rob's mother. She met with her husband behind closed doors and then emerged some time later to announce their decision.

Looking at me, she said, "You can sleep under this roof, but you will be in the room next to ours, Ben will be upstairs, and my husband will keep watch, praise the Lord."

What the hell did she think, I asked myself. That we were going to sneak out of their house and have sex somewhere? If we had wanted to do that, we had 2,500 miles behind us that could have provided endless opportunities.

After a couple of days, Rob's mother brought up, in a roundabout way, the subject of going home.

"Praise the Lord, have you ever been on an airplane?" she asked me.

It was clear to me that she thought we should end this crazy adventure, come to our senses, and return home to our parents.

Ben and I hadn't talked about what we were going to do once we got there or where we were going next. Summer was coming to an end soon, and I knew I had to finish school. Ben weighed his options and didn't come up with much, and we were running out of money. So we decided to consider going home. We stayed for another week, hiking in the desert, exploring saguaro cactus and the fabricated village of Old Tucson, before boarding a plane that took us to New York's Kennedy Airport. I arrived home with fifty cents in my pocket and was greeted with the welcome my mother had promised me.

I walked in the front door, dirty and tired and carrying, in addition to a heavy backpack, experiences no one in my family could ever realize. Liz stood at the kitchen sink, turned around, and said, "Feed the cat, please."

I felt like I had just arrived at someone else's home. It was familiar, but not something that belonged to me anymore, nor something of which I wanted to be a part. As soon as I could, I promised myself, I would leave for good.

Left Turn

Everything will be OK in the end; if it's not OK, it's not the end.

—Author unknown

Mike was late.

"If he isn't here by nine, I'm going alone," I said to Mom on a Saturday evening later that same year. I was standing on the stairs leading up to the bedrooms dressed in a beige knit turtleneck with trumpet sleeves and blue jeans that were snug enough to reveal the outline of my slim teenage body. My long hair was neatly coifed and flowed a few inches past my shoulders and my makeup had been carefully applied just moments earlier.

My sister and her boyfriend were hosting a party at his parents' house, and I planned to go with my friend Mike. Mike was a twin, and his brother Mark was slightly cuter, but Mike and I spent a lot of time together, and eventually we became good friends. He said he'd be there around 8:30 to pick me up, but by nine he hadn't arrived, so I decided to go by myself. Besides, I loved driving my '73 Volkswagen Beetle. It was my first car, and I bought it with $500 I borrowed from Mom two months before.

Earlier that afternoon, I'd taken it out for a drive, heading west on Route 80 out of New Jersey and into Pennsylvania, going as far as my spirit wanted to take my Beetle buddy and me. It was late November, and the autumn hues had already begun to fade from the landscape. The air was cold and dry, but I cracked the windows open slightly anyway to feel the late autumn chill and exhilarating sense of freedom sweep across my face. It was in that moment that I felt completely free. I was in control of me. The tension and confinement I often felt at home peeled off my skin from the wind blowing through the car, and I could finally take a deep breath. I wanted to feel this way forever.

I loved that little car. I had just made the first insurance payment on it and felt oh so grown-up. It was Miami blue with fog lights on the back bumper and a big orange button on the dashboard, though I'm not sure what that was for. Even though Dad had a Beetle, he warned me not to get one. They were, after all, fragile little cars with not much structure. One swift back draft off the tail of a semi on the interstate would send the car swerving into the adjacent lane.

"If you get in an accident, the person who will get hurt is you," Dad warned me.

Of course, at seventeen I knew how much smarter I was than either of my parents, so I thanked him for his advice and bought it anyway. If it gave me a means to get out of the house and away from the drama, I would take it.

My appearance that night wasn't overstated, I thought; just enough to maybe help me get lucky later. Mom was in her usual chocolate-brown swivel chair in front of the television. Swiveling made it easy for her to spin around and reach for her cocktail, which she did often. Her beverage of choice was a Manhattan, and when that one was empty, she headed to the kitchen for a refill. When the pitcher of them was drained, she made another batch. I guess I came by it honestly, what with all those Saturday night high school parties when I stumbled in the door trying to hide my alcohol-induced unsteadiness. Either she didn't notice because of her own condition, or she'd given up on me. But this Saturday night I was sober. Hoping to get lucky later with Mike, my sex partner of choice for the evening, I figured the partying would start when I got there.

My intense interest in sex was borne more out of curiosity than a primal hunger. As much as I wanted her to, my mother had never had the talk with me, and it left me wondering what the big mystery was.

"You're too young," she said each time I asked.

At each milestone of development, I heard the same excuse.

"You're too young."

When I began developing breasts, I was too young. When I started menstruating, I was too young. When I developed crushes on boys, I was still too young. One night when I was about thirteen years old, she told me to wait for her in my room, she wanted to talk. Finally, I'd hear all about it. This thing they call sex and what it's all about. I just wanted to know. So I waited with the anticipation of a twelve-year-old boy ready to steal his dad's girlie magazines after he fell asleep. I was happy that my mother finally saw me as a growing young woman and respected me enough to share this sacred secret. I even excitedly whispered to Liz that I was finally going to know about it. The mysteries of the adult world and what went on behind bedroom doors would finally be revealed to me.

I sat on my bed and waited. And waited. Mom never came.

Disappointed for the last time, I decided then that I'd find out on my own. My mother either wasn't comfortable with the topic or didn't respect me enough to think I deserved to know. She wasn't aware that I'd been curious for a long time. Before I developed any visible sex characteristics, I would stand naked in front of the mirror behind my locked bedroom door and stare at the androgynous figure in the mirror, wondering if I was a girl or a boy because I had never seen the naked body of either. So

I stopped asking. I decided to take sex education into my own hands through on-the-job training and, as a teenage girl, finding an available partner was no problem.

The route to my sister's boyfriend's house was pretty straight forward until the state highway. I reached a fork in the road that gave me a choice of direction. If I turned right, I could enter the highway at a traffic light, turn left to go east, and drive for a short distance until making a right turn into the neighborhood. If I turned left, I could follow a road that led me straight across the highway into the neighborhood. Highway systems at the time often had grass medians with occasional breaks for crossing traffic. Since I wasn't exactly sure where to turn right if I choose the first option, I turned left. This assured me a straight shot across into the neighborhood.

I drove up to the stop sign at the edge of the highway. At 9:15, it was dark and Jersey-cold, but otherwise dry and clear. From the left was the westbound traffic, from the right was traffic heading east. The spot in the road where the crossing occurred at the median was at the chasm of a downhill that came together from both directions, so cars coming from either east or west had plenty of acceleration power. I looked east for oncoming traffic and saw that it was clear, then across to the median in the middle, and began to move forward.

I rolled into the median and something white-bright caught my eye. My head and torso whirled to the right. In what seemed like an instant, I saw headlights at the passenger door. Out of instinct, I threw my hands up over my face, fingers spread, palms facing away, recoiling. Then, blackness.

To this day, I don't remember the impact. It was hammered out of my memory at that moment, and it would be months before sporadic memories began returning in violent flashbacks, like the split-second appearance of images spliced into a motion picture. It's called post-trauma amnesia; I call it a blessing. The violence to the body created by the force of one car slamming into another at high speed, of being catapulted through a steel door, the sound of tires screeching, car frames crunching, glass shattering, and bones breaking has no place in the human psyche. Our minds have an incredible ability to protect us, and I'm grateful for that.

What I do know—from witnesses and police reports—was that the impact from the other car threw me out the driver's door like a rag doll onto the highway. I didn't hear the window shattering as my head went through it. I didn't feel my body landing on the road. I don't know how long I was unconscious. The entire event was wiped from my consciousness until the following year, when flashbacks allowed me to piece together some of what happened. I remembered waking up lying on the road. Through hazy vision, I saw the night sky and a crowd of people standing around me in a circle. I saw the flashing lights of the ambulance in my peripheral vision. I didn't move because I couldn't. Someone took off his coat and laid it over me. I didn't feel the cold. I didn't feel the pain.

I continued to float in and out of consciousness for several days. Bits of memory continued to make its way back into my mind—feeling the movement of the ambulance as the medic was shouting *"What's your phone number?!"* Lying on the gurney in the emergency room, the foggy images of my family standing nearby—Liz, Joey, Mom, Dad, and Liz's boyfriend, Dave—faded in and out. Feeling the neurosurgeon brush the bottom of my foot with a feather to check for paralysis. All of this faded in and out. Then, I awoke again to see the steel-gray x-ray equipment hovering over me to look inside my broken body.

When all was said and done, I had bruised kidneys, a broken right tibia, shattered pelvis, broken finger on my right hand, broken jaw, and fractured second cervical vertebrae, the C-2. The Hangman's fracture. This is when extreme trauma creates sudden hyperextension of the upper spine, causing the upper part of the cervical spine (skull, C1, and C2) to laterally shift away from the lower portion of the spine. This must have happened when I whirled to the right a split second before impact, and my head was thrown back through the driver's side window, also causing my brain to be thrown against the back side of my skull.

I stayed in the intensive care unit for several days, my surroundings drifting in and out of a haze, like trying to focus a scene through the viewfinder of a camera. Painkillers can be merciful in their ability to spare a more visceral memory. After being thrown from the car, I came to a stop on my back with my head turned to the right, and that's how the paramedics stabilized me until my injuries could be assessed. Neck stabilization was still relatively primitive at the time. Sandbags were placed around my head and neck to keep them immobile. More were laid close to my right hip and up and down my right leg. Since my head was still turned to the right, I couldn't see the door to the left of my bed that led out to the hallway.

Every now and then, someone would appear next to my bed, and I'd sense their presence and open my eyes. I had a constant pain in the back of my head like a thousand sharp needles piercing my scalp, and whenever I awoke, I'd cry out. A nurse eventually came over with a vacuum hose and suctioned what was left of the driver's side window out of my skull. The sound was like that of suctioning gravel off a tile floor, but it was coming from *inside* my head. When the noise stopped, the pain stopped.

Treatment protocol was to remain on my back for six months with cables attached to my forehead, hanging down the back of the bed, and leading to a set of weights near the floor that would ensure no movement of the spine. But the halo head brace was a new device on the market, and my doctors thought it might be a good alternative to long-term traction. It arrived three days later, but by then the bones in my spine had begun to heal, and my head was stuck in the right-turn position. A nurse approached the bed, placed her hands on either side of my head, picked it up off the pillow, and began straightening it. I screamed. She stopped. A moment later, she tried again. Again, I screamed.

"I'll do it!" I cried.

"All right, but you have one hour," she said. She turned on her heel and left.

Little by little, with both of my hands now cradling my head, I re-straightened my crooked neck, making micro moves at a time. Each time, I felt a grinding sensation in my neck that came with intense pain that at this point saw no relief from the drugs.

I was just about done when several people came into the room carrying what looked like a robotic device. It was the halo head brace, and it required a team of doctors to "install" it. They congratulated me, telling me I was the first person on the East Coast to wear it. The head gear consisted of a large metal ring with sterile pins running cross-directionally through it, like a small bicycle wheel with four spokes aiming in toward the center. These were the pins that screwed into my skull, a half inch above the outer edges of the eyebrows and a half inch above the ears. The frame was somewhat movable and attached to a fiberglass vest that covered my torso front and back.

Topless and propped up in my bed, I remained motionless while the team went to work. My long hair was spared and only shaved where the pins screwed into the skull above my ears. The doctors first checked the position of the pins relative to my skull, and then they manually tightened them until they made contact with the skin. Next, they used a torque wrench to tighten the pins contra laterally—one doctor working the front left pin while the other worked the back right pin, then they switched—front right and back left. This continued until each site recorded eight-inch pounds of torque. When the last pin was in place and the vest fitted around my torso, my direct line of vision was slightly to the right, and this is how my vertebrae healed. The original model of the halo was large and cumbersome and created a sense of top-heaviness when it was worn.

After eight days in the ICU, I was moved into a regular room. It was my eighteenth birthday.

Before the accident, I had asked my parents for a set of skis. I often went downhill skiing on the weekends and was a member of my high school ski club. I learned to slalom and loved to see how fast I could fly over the moguls. The thrill of the speed was such a rush. Now I lay immobile, surrounded by hardware, just wanting my body back in one piece.

It was unusual to see my entire family in the same room together. I suppose this crisis created a temporary truce between my parents. My parents, brother, and sister stood around my bed as I sat propped in a semi-reclined position. Pillows supported me from behind and on the sides so the weight of the halo would not cause me to fall to the side and into the bed rails, which were always in the upright position. The amount of pain medicine had been reduced, creating the dubious effect of better mental coherence but more awareness of the pain, which was constant. It didn't come from the broken bones but seemed to migrate from my entire body, especially where the screws entered my skull. They had to penetrate deep enough to ensure no movement. Betadine ointment oozing from the pins' points of contact added to its unsightliness and gave the appearance of open wounds puncturing my skull. I woke most nights from the sound of myself moaning.

My mother handed me a long, narrow gift-wrapped box that was like the type that held a bracelet from a jewelry store. With help, I removed the wrapping and opened the box. Inside was a set of Barbie doll–sized skis with a note that read "Happy Birthday. Love, Mom and Dad."

The irony of the moment made me laugh.

"The real ones are home, waiting for you," Mom said.

"I don't think skiing is in my plans this year, Ma." But I appreciated the gift, especially considering that my parents usually didn't collaborate on anything together.

I had a team of doctors—a neurosurgeon, orthopedic surgeon, urologist, and internist. The orthopedist chose not to wire my jaw shut, but I was still restricted to a liquid diet. Anything that could be sucked through a straw was allowed. My food was blended, juiced, pulverized, and squeezed. Even with all the milkshakes (some of them spilling down the front of my vest), I still lost twenty-five pounds.

My neurosurgeon entered my room one morning when Mom was there.

"Will I be able to tap dance when I'm better?" I asked him.

"Of course," he replied.

"Great. I've always wanted to," I said.

He and Mom laughed.

My friends from school came every day. Mary Pat, who lived three houses down from me, was there a lot. I slept often and woke up to find her sitting next to my bed, reading or doing homework. She came most days after school, always staying until I woke up. It's no wonder she became a nurse later in life; her capacity for compassion was unusual for a teenage girl.

Eventually, I was strong enough to transfer from my bed to a wheelchair. This allowed me a new level of freedom, and I often went exploring up and down the hallways. When there wasn't much foot traffic, I'd see how fast I could wheel myself from one end of the hall to the other. Another older teen had been admitted to my floor, and I was glad to have someone to spend time with after visiting hours ended and my friends went home. He was a bit of a rebel, just the type I was attracted to, and our nightly drag racing in wheelchairs was a much-needed cure for my growing boredom.

Each morning, an orderly came to deliver me to the rehab unit, where I practiced walking as I held onto parallel bars. Because of the weight of the halo brace, the decision was made to not add any more weight by putting casts on my leg and hip. Most of my weight was held up by my left arm since a metal pin had been inserted into the right pinky finger and stuck out a quarter inch. Pain would travel up my right leg into my hip each time I put weight on that side, so my movements were slow and methodical. Every other step, I shifted my weight from my left leg to my right, slowly leaning onto that side, bracing for another electric current to travel up my right side.

I had abandoned my meditation practicing before my cross-country trip with Ben earlier that year. We were traveling the open road, and I didn't think there was much opportunity to sit twice a day in silence while trying to make it to our next destination. There in the hospital, I had nothing but time, so as I lay in bed at night, I closed my eyes and repeated my mantram, hoping it would help my mind focus on something other than the constant pain. Having something on which to focus my attention other than my hurting body helped to get me through some very long nights, and it was nice to get back to my practice. It also provided a small sense of empowerment in my otherwise helpless state.

Five days before Christmas, I was allowed to go home. With walking cane in hand, I was wheeled to the hospital entrance, where my parents' car, filled with flowers, stuffed animals, cards, and candy, sat idling. Dad helped me out of my wheelchair and into the backseat of their white sedan and drove home slowly enough to match the pace of anyone who might have been walking alongside.

There was a revolving door of visitors at home as well. My teachers came with books and homework so I wouldn't fall further behind. Neighbors brought food. My ex-boyfriend Gary came often, spending many nights sitting on the sofa with me, playing board games, or just keeping me company. One of my friends from school came by and told me that another classmate had witnessed the accident and raced up the road to call for an ambulance, getting a speeding ticket in the process. Even Paul, who broke my heart earlier that year, came by with a gift. It was a reproduction of a painting that depicted a lake and farmhouse and reminded me of a special place we had gone swimming during our brief romance earlier that spring.

I was supposed to wear the halo brace for eight weeks and couldn't wait to get it off. Its top heaviness made moving around difficult (I had to be extremely careful on stairs); the only sleeping position was on my back; and because of the hard plastic body brace it was attached to, which prevented me from bathing, I smelled bad. Around week six, I had a follow-up appointment with my neurosurgeon. He was a friendly man who poked around the areas where the screws penetrated my head, making small talk with my mother.

"Well, little lady, so how long have you been wearing this?"

"Eight weeks," I blurted out.

"Eight weeks already, eh? Well, then I think it's time we take it off!"

I didn't say anything.

Removing the brace required an overnight stay in the hospital. I was admitted a few days later on the same floor where I had stayed. That evening, two doctors and a nurse came into my room, one of them carrying a toolbox. As I sat up, they pulled the curtain around my bed for privacy and proceeded to remove the loose-fitting shirt I was wearing. Unlike when the brace was installed, this time I was fully aware of my nakedness and every painful sensation associated with the hardware being disassembled from my head.

The vertical metal rods that connected the body brace to the metal head gear were loosened first, and then the hard plastic and very smelly harness was removed and set aside. That was the easy part. Next, the doctors reached into their toolbox, took out their wrenches, and began loosening each pin in opposite order from how it was installed until all four pins had retracted from my skull. I let out a cry as a loud *clank!* indicated that the pins and ring were in their final stage of removal and the remaining hardware was pulled off. Drugs would have been helpful.

I stayed in the hospital overnight for observation and went home the next morning wearing a soft collar around my neck.

At the end of January, I returned to school. Without a car to drive, I resumed riding the school bus, which was okay because a level of subliminal fear still lingered just below the surface of my awareness, and getting into a car—anyone's car—made me tremble.

Any kind of spinal injury can have lifelong effects, even when there is no paralysis. But when the damage occurs in the cervical spine, that's when it becomes life-threatening. I learned that the farther up the spine the point of injury is, the greater the threat.

The fact that I wasn't paralyzed in the accident is miraculous. My injury was considered a fracture, not a complete break. When a break happens, nerves can easily be severed and paralysis or death is the final sentence handed down. For reasons that could not be apparent to me then, I was spared. I know others who were not. "There but for the grace of God go I." These words have become my new mantram.

Even though I have no cognitive recollection of the impact, the memory became stored in my body. We are programmed to survive, and during an initial threat, our body's survival mechanism—the sympathetic nervous system, also known as "fight, flight, or freeze"—kicks in, releasing a surge of stress hormones to activate us to flee from danger. Known as "cell memory" or "body memory," it's what can develop into posttraumatic stress disorder if the original experience is not processed in a safe environment, such as with a trusted therapist.

Victims of childhood abuse and returning war veterans know this very well. Once referred to as "shell shock," PTSD is what happens when a person reacts to a stimulus as though the trauma is happening at that moment. Since the body has no sense of time, it can't know that the original trauma may have happened years, or even decades, before. When a trigger occurs, such as a sound, memory, smell, or image, the body immediately goes into sympathetic response. Cognitively, we know there is no danger. But, viscerally, our bodies—and, therefore, our fear network—become overwhelmed. For years when I talked about the accident, my body began to tremble and it was difficult to breath, and I felt like I was suffocating. It's as though—to a lesser degree—I was experiencing it again.

Today I'm acutely aware of how each detail of that Saturday night, each seemingly innocuous decision—wait for Mike or go alone, turn left at the intersection or turn right—altered the trajectory of my life.

In the years since then, with the benefit of hindsight, I can more clearly see that night through the lens of life experience. I came to believe that I had to be able to walk. I had to remain independent. God couldn't take away my legs, even though He would later take so much else.

Physically, I would remain whole.

Leaving

*You can't get away from yourself by moving
from one place to another.*

—Ernest Hemingway

I met Walter while I was still in high school. He was my media teacher and twice my age. After the accident when I returned to school in January of my senior year, I was told that without completing the work I had missed, I would not graduate. So I met with Walter every day in the small office behind his classroom for tutoring, and by late spring, I had developed a serious crush. Because I was still in high school, I kept a distance, but that didn't get in the way of my growing obsession with him. He gave the speech at my graduation, and when I marched past the stage in my cap and gown, I glanced up and saw him smiling at me. Not just any smile; this one had mutual attraction written all over it that tickled my bones.

A few days later I made what felt like a bold move. I picked up the phone and called him. We talked for a long time, me telling him about the plastic surgery I had the day before to close up the holes the halo brace had left in my head. He then asked, "Can you put a helmet on?"

I laughed. "Of course I can!" I sensed where this line of questioning was going, and my heart skipped a few beats.

"Do you want to go for a ride on my motorcycle?"

I wanted to shout *YES!* but managed to coolly reply, "Sure, that would be fun."

He picked me up an hour later, and we rode up into the hills of northern New Jersey and went swimming in a secluded reservoir, and by the end of the day, I knew I was in love.

We stopped at a roadside café for dinner on the way back, and I took a seat across the table from him. Walter looked at me and smiled, his expression lingering for more than a minute, and I knew he had feelings for me as well. Our relationship quickly shifted from teacher-student to lovers, a status I tried to keep hidden from my mother. That is, until the morning she called his house after I lied and said I was staying at my friend Denise's the night before.

Denise was one of the few friends who didn't leave me once I went public with my relationship with Walter. We had been best friends since kindergarten and were practically inseparable. She didn't know about my little lie I told Mom but neither did she hold it against me after I confessed to her what I had done. Denise had an innocence that drew me to her; it made me feel safe in my topsy-turvy world in which I was living. We both started our friendship with the same purity and virtue, but as we grew into adolescence, and my path diverted toward a more reckless horizon; she didn't waver. She stayed my friend.

Mom, on the other hand, had a difficult time accepting that her defiant eighteen-year-old daughter was bedding down with a man who was thirty-five years old and the father of a young child. When she first found out, she declared, "In this house, we don't sleep with our boyfriends."

Earlier that summer, Mom drove to Ithaca for a high school reunion and was gone for several days. Liz later overheard her whispering on the phone to her friend about a man she met.

So when she made her declaration of no sleeping with boyfriends, I replied, "Oh really? Does that rule apply to everyone in this house?"

She shot a glare at me that revealed both anger and embarrassment. That was the end of that rule.

I began spending even less time at home and more time at Walter's house, and Mom asked me why I was there so often.

I said, "If you had a choice between living where the tension is as thick as mud or where you can love freely, what would you choose?"

"You're lucky. You have a choice," she answered.

"So do you, Mom. You just don't realize it."

One evening after she was well oiled, Mom came into my room, pulled up a chair, and sat down facing me sitting on my bed.

"You're a whore," she said.

"Get out of my room," I shot back.

"No, it's my house and I can be here."

"Get OUT of my room!"

"YOU get out."

So I did.

A year after graduation, I left home and took my heart with me. I got a secretarial job that paid well and could afford to live on my own, and I soon found an apartment three towns away. It was the second floor of an old Victorian house two blocks from downtown Morristown. I took up jogging to be more like my dad, and in the evenings I covered several laps on the high school track across the street. The neighborhood was sketchy, but I hardly noticed because I was tasting the sweet flavor of real freedom once again.

Distance (time, as well as geographic) does wonders for gaining clarity. After I knew my exodus provided a much-needed buffer, I settled into my own life and removed myself from Mom's influence.

I began to take stock of how both of my parents fit into my life. I began to see more clearly how my mother's unhappiness with her marriage played against my relationship with my father. She hated him, so Liz and I were taught to as well. Like a frog who can't feel the temperature rise in the pot of water he's jumped into, unaware that he is slowly boiling, I hadn't recognized during those years the gradual deterioration of the relationship I once had with my father at the hands of my mother.

Now that I had an apartment and was living on my own, I could set the terms of my relationship with Mom. Phone calls were acceptable, but only before 8 p.m., before the alcohol she had been nursing for hours took over her manners, her mouth, and her sense of dignity. Weekend visits were welcome, occasional dinner invitations extended and received with gratitude. I was leading a grown-up life and having a grown-up relationship with both my parents. This could work, I thought. My relationship with Walter was also getting stronger, so after a year I gave up my apartment and moved in with him.

The little house where we lived was a converted summer cabin, much smaller than my apartment in Morristown. It sat hidden among trees at the end of a narrow and winding road on top of a hill in a tired wooded lake community. The motif was mid-1970s, complete with white resin furniture and red shag carpet. Cheap paneling that I nicknamed "Kodak board" because of its paper thinness covered the walls. The main room in the center of the house had a large stone fireplace that often served as the only heat source in the winter. The kitchen was almost large enough for two people, and the bathroom was half that size with a corner shower enclosure, toilet, and small sink with the pipes visible underneath. The room that served as the bedroom was in the front of the house. A picture window opened to a view of the woods and a gravel driveway, and a much smaller second bedroom was next to the bathroom. It was quite small, but at the time it didn't matter. Happiness had finally arrived on my doorstep, I was in love, and all seemed right with my world.

Walter and I spent all of our time together. In winter, we went cross-country skiing at the snow-covered golf course down the road, racing against the wind along the tracks left by snowmobilers. I taught him how to play racquetball and how to downhill ski at Hunter Mountain. We spent one bitter cold weekend at a bed and breakfast in Vermont, skiing in the powdery snow and staying warm drinking wine by the fire at night. In summer, we drove to North Carolina's Outer Banks and camped in his van on the beach. I sat on the back of his motorcycle, my arms wrapped around his waist, as we sped along the beach, slaloming in and out of the surf. We went crabbing off a pier on Ocracoke Island and cooked them in an open fire pit. We hiked the Appalachian Trail one winter and camped in a pup tent, warming our freeze-dried beef stroganoff over a one-burner stove in our tent as the snow fell outside. For Christmas that year, he gave me a kit to make my own snowsuit. I was beginning to believe that this is what real family is about.

Loss

*We numb our minds and heart so one need not be
broken and the other need not be bothered.*

—Peggy Haymes

It was Saturday morning in early August the following year. I was
lying in bed, suspended in a light dream state, when I heard the
phone ring in the periphery of my awareness. I felt Walter stir and
climb out of bed, his barefoot patter disappearing down the hall.
I glanced with one eye at the clock on the table; it read 7:00. Still
groggy, I heard myself say, "Something's wrong" as I began to drift
back to sleep. Walter came back a moment later. Still sleepy, he
said, "It's your mom."

Half awake, I pulled myself out of bed, down the hall, and
into the kitchen, where the phone receiver was waiting on a nearby
table. I picked it up. My mother's voice, monotone and lifeless,
came through the wire.

"Sue, come home. Liz died last night."

A scream erupted from deep inside me. I dropped the phone,
ran into the living room, and fell into Walter, who was running
toward me. He caught me and carried me to the sofa. There he
held me, our naked bodies wrapped around each other, rocking,
rocking, as I cried. His young daughter heard the commotion and

came out of her room. She said nothing as she stood watching us, not understanding what just happened.

My sister was dead, and I had to go home. I didn't want to, even in the wake of this tragedy, because I was afraid to allow myself to come anywhere near the fold of my parents' lives.

I slowly got dressed and made the three-mile drive to the house by the river. Dad was downstairs in the laundry room when I walked in. I ran up and threw my arms around his neck, at which point he said with a curious lack of emotion, "It happened last night." That was Dad, poker-faced to the core.

In the kitchen, Mom was sitting in her chair near the window, still wearing the clothes she had on from the night before, wringing her hands as her tears fell.

I looked out the window and paused at the scene: the river was still flowing, tree branches were still swaying, cars were still driving by in the distance. The world outside curiously went on, oblivious to the tectonic shift that had just occurred in our lives. I knelt at Mom's feet and took her hands and stayed there for what seemed like a very long time.

Through her tears, Mom said, "I'd cry just as much if it had been you, Sue."

Her voice—like her heart—was broken.

"Don't, Mom. I know, I know," I said. *Please stop*, I thought. This scene was beyond my understanding, and I wanted to *run*.

What became more curious than my father's lack of emotion was my own. He was always that way, even-keeled and hard to read. But I was typically all over the map emotionally and wore my emotions so much that an old boyfriend once said, "Hell, even Helen Keller could tell how you're feeling."

The initial shock of hearing the news that morning soon wore off. *Was this normal*, I wondered? *Why don't I feel anything?* Since I had never lost anyone close before, protocol for acceptable behavior in this moment in time was lost on me.

Eventually, I stood up and looked down at Mom, still wringing her hands. "I'm going home to get some things," I said. I knew I had to be with my family during the unfamiliar process of making calls, ordering flowers, planning a funeral, burying my sister, and readjusting to a life without her.

I wasn't sure what I was feeling; it was more like a non-feeling. I had already emotionally detached myself from my family and still felt the sting of the battles Liz and I had while growing up. Years before, when Mom sat me down one afternoon and said, "Liz is sick. She has an illness. We have to help her," I found it difficult to feel empathy.

Anorexia and bulimia weren't yet household terms; I only knew that Liz was too skinny. At 5'6", she had been a plump one hundred forty pounds in eighth grade. As a high school senior, she was seventy-five pounds and still dropping. She had the appearance of a skeleton draped in skin. Somewhere in between her extreme weights, she had been most beautiful. Her high cheekbones, round deep-brown eyes, and auburn hair set her apart from other girls her age. They were pretty, but she was stunning. But her beauty melted away as fast as her weight, and by the time she graduated high school, her eyes, surrounded by darkly pigmented skin, had sunk deep into her skull. She had stopped menstruating, and every joint protruded from her body. The only meat left on her was the silicon breasts she had implanted with money she saved from her weekend waitressing job.

Liz also drank. A *lot*. Mom found empty vodka bottles stuffed under cushions, behind furniture, on the closet floor under her clothes. Mom insisted she see a therapist. Liz lied to him. She said she wasn't drinking anymore, but she was. She said she wasn't vomiting anymore, but she was. Mom took her to a doctor who admitted her to the hospital in the self-care unit. This is where they put people who weren't sick enough to stay in bed. Here, she wore her street clothes instead of the hospital-regulation thin cotton open-backed gowns. She could walk the halls and get food out of the community refrigerator. She was required to eat six meals a day to increase her weight, and the hospital unit made sure food was readily available to the patients.

Liz's high school graduation

I went with my family on one of their evening visits, and Liz sat on her bed, busying herself with books or papers or games or anything that would serve as a distraction from the elephant in the room, from the embarrassment she must have felt by the spotlight that was now aimed at her illness. The level of effort I put forth to have a conversation was equal to hers. By then, I didn't care very much.

Or maybe I just didn't understand. So I sat and waited for the visit to end. After two weeks and a ten-pound weight gain, she was allowed to come home. Mom told her that she needed to reach one hundred pounds or she wouldn't be allowed to go to college. To Liz, who graduated summa cum laude of her private girls' school and served as valedictorian at graduation, this was unthinkable. By mid-summer, her weight crept up to ninety-five pounds. She left for school in August.

Liz could also be mean. *Very* mean. Before she got sick, her venomous tongue was quick to strike, and I didn't know how to fight back. She had an off-the-charts intellect, and her blows were of the cerebral kind that I wasn't fast or witty enough to rebut. So I quietly grew to hate her. I continued to separate myself from my parents' world and added her to my personal list of estranged family members. As we got older and her illness developed, she mellowed, and I'll admit that she tried harder to bridge the gap between us, while I was more reluctant to do so. Liz was still an active member of Team Mom, and by then I had quit that sport.

I could eventually forgive how she treated me, but it was hard to witness the pain she caused Mom. It wasn't intentional, but it still stung. In addition to lying to her doctors, she was also lying to Mom, and they both knew it. Although she swore she wasn't drinking or vomiting, I knew she was because she had mastered the art of the "secret hurl."

After I moved out, I occasionally went home for dinner. Just as when I was growing up, I still shared in kitchen clean-up duty. I stood at the sink washing dishes and handed them off to Liz for drying. One time as I stood at the sink, she disappeared out of my peripheral vision so I turned around. There I saw her, crouched over the garbage can near the pantry, emptying the contents of her stomach without making a sound.

One Tuesday, Mom asked if the three of us could have a girls' dinner out soon. We planned to meet at Mom's that Thursday, and when I arrived at the house, Liz had been in her room with the door closed for a long time. Mom stood at the door, knocking and calling for her.

"Liz, let me in, please. Sue's here and we're leaving."

When Liz eventually opened the door, Mom stood staring at a very intoxicated girl.

Liz wavered on her feet, staring past Mom at nothing in particular, pretending in her best effort to appear normal when she suddenly lost her equilibrium and fell toward Mom. Trying to prop Liz up, Mom turned to me with a pained expression and said, "Dinner's canceled."

That was the last time I ever saw my sister.

Later that night, after Liz had sobered somewhat, Mom held her in her arms as she lay on the sofa, weeping.

"I'm sick, and I'm scared," she cried.

The following evening, Liz sat on the sofa in the living room across from Mom's swivel chair where Joey was sitting. His back was turned to her as he watched television when something caught his awareness and he turned to see her slumping on the sofa. He yelled for Dad, who was in the next room. Dad ran into the living room, saw her, and ran upstairs to wake Mom. She flew down the stairs as Dad scooped Liz into his arms, handing her to Mom as they practically dove into the car. As Dad sped to the hospital a quarter mile away, Mom propped Liz in her lap in the passenger seat, attempting to give her mouth-to-mouth. Her chest would not rise. Mom saw her eyes glaze over and cried, "Joe, she's gone!"

Unable to revive her in the emergency room, the doctor pronounced her dead sometime around 9:30 p.m.

She was twenty-one years old.

The week following Liz's death while I stayed at my parents' house, I lay awake in the guest room at night and listened to my mother, upstairs in Liz's room, talking to her. I couldn't quite hear her words, but her pain was palpable. I lay frozen, breathing shallow, not able to *begin* to understand her grief.

Dear God, I thought. I hope I *never* have to know that level of suffering.

The Heart That Cries

Nothing is so painful to the human mind
as a great and sudden change.

—Mary Shelley

The year following Liz's death, I turned twenty-one. Walter planned a surprise party for me. My parents and Joey came, our close friends came. Everyone who meant something to me was there. And in spite of a palpable awareness of Liz's absence, Mom almost seemed to be enjoying herself. Although I could see the sadness hidden behind her eyes and hear the sorrow through her laughter, sharing this celebration together was still a refreshing change. I had put Liz behind me, or so I thought. I didn't visit her grave. I kept nothing that had belonged to her. There were to be no reminders. Life was in front of me, and that's where I kept my sights. Being near my mother in her grief was uncomfortable and, since I hadn't grieved, I couldn't identify with her pain. Watching her socialize settled my anxiety. It lightened the atmosphere.

At one point in the evening, Walter called for everyone's attention. I stood humbled as he poured champagne and, along with everyone, raised a glass to my formal entry into adulthood. His eyes glowed and his smile melted me. Much later, after the party was over and everyone had long gone home, the house was quiet. Walter had gone to bed, and I was closing up for the night.

I saw on the table a small wrapped gift with my name on the tag. I opened it to find a gray wool cap. It was a simple gift, a gesture that spoke of his thoughtfulness. I needed something to keep me warm when we skied and hiked in the cold northeast winters, and this was a perfect accessory. But it was more than I needed. My party was the best gift I could imagine. I would lock it into my memory, and it would be decades before I knew its true value.

The next day was my actual birthday, and Mom had flowers delivered to my office. Had she done this in my teenage years, when I was in such a hurry to grow up and told myself that I no longer needed her, I would have been embarrassed and somewhat miffed at her public sentiment. But not now. Now, I was proud to be her daughter and had no objections to any expression of love she wanted to exhibit. I called her and told her how much I loved her. I remember feeling it, really *feeling* it. Expressing it freely and openly and with an emotional abandon that I had, until recently, kept locked away. The years of estranging myself from her, of convincing myself that I didn't need her, or anyone, were behind me. I loved her like I had when I was twelve, when we sat on my bed for hours at night, talking. She would tell me that I could do anything in life, that I could be anything I wanted. My adolescent insecurities didn't allow me to completely believe her, but it was still nice to know my mom was my best advocate. I needed my mother so desperately then. And years later, when I had finally crossed the chasm of teenage rebellion and reappeared slightly more mature, I admitted to myself that I still needed her.

However, something began to chafe at me after Liz died. When she was alive, I had an intuitive sense that she would not always be in my life. I didn't dwell on the thought but found it hard to ignore the constant feeling of her simply being gone. When I pictured my life in the future, Liz was nowhere in it. I just felt a void. Fate proved me right when she died. I now had the same feeling about my mother, and it terrified me.

Liz died a week before she and Mom were to move out. One month later, Mom left. She moved into the deserted home of a friend who had abruptly left the country. It was a beautiful, expansive modern house that sat on eighteen acres along the river, complete with sunken living room, swimming pool, and horse stables. The owners literally left in the middle of the night, and the house remained as it had been since then. It was cavernous, and I imagined Mom's voice echoing through the halls during her nightly one-sided conversations with Liz.

In spite of an enormous void that remained, Mom tried to bring a sense of normalcy to her shattered life. She got a roommate. She went to work. She threw parties. And she drank. A *lot*. I supposed she filled her void the only way she knew how: to pour alcohol into it.

By all accounts, she crawled into a bottle and didn't come out.

That terrifying feeling continued to grow in me, and I began to back away. The undefined sense that had relentlessly gnawed at my gut about Liz had returned uninvited and, although I knew Mom needed me, I was afraid. I began to again distance myself from her, and she felt it. It must have felt to her like losing both daughters, only my departure was by choice. I told myself that if I didn't let myself love her, it wouldn't hurt so much when she died. I could emotionally divorce myself from her now, and that would lessen the grief later on.

"Can you stay with me?" she asked on Christmas Eve the year Liz died.

Heavy snow had fallen, and I reasoned that the roads would be impassable. Part truth, part excuse.

"I'm stuck here," I told her as I looked around my bungalow living room. Walter didn't have a stocking for me, so he pinned one of my socks to the fireplace mantle and filled it with chocolate. I looked at it for a few moments. I wanted to stay. I didn't doubt that Mom loved me, but my fear of losing her, coupled with her resentment over my reconciliation with Dad, helped justify staying away. Walter's love, on the other hand, didn't appear to have any strings attached. I simply felt more at home with him.

"I'll have Dad pick you up."

"No, I'll be there tomorrow."

For the first and only time in her life, my mother spent Christmas Eve by herself. She never understood why I stayed away. How could I explain to her that I needed immunity from my fractured family? That Liz was gone and, therefore, so was her ally and I couldn't risk being pulled back into the theatrics? That in spite of all this, I was terribly afraid of losing her and, out of misguided fear, thought that it was better I keep my distance?

My self-imposed estrangement worked for a while until it became too difficult to ignore the pain it was causing. She was hurting, and I was responsible, at least for my part of it. I eventually came to terms with the fear and resolved to embrace her like I truly wanted to. I reasoned that, even if she died, we would have had this time together. She needed it; and, truth be told, so did I. My selfishness had caused enough hardship for my family, regardless of whether or not it was motivated by self-preservation. So I began spending more time with Mom. I visited more often, sometimes dropping by unannounced. Seeing Mom smile when I arrived brought much-needed healing to us both. And Dad also found reasons to drop by her house, whether to deliver the Sunday paper, to have pancakes, or just to see how she was holding up.

Mom and Dad reconciled the following March. She moved back home (Joey had opted to stay with Dad), and they began to rebuild their long-abandoned marriage. They went out with their friends. They worked on house projects that had been neglected for years. They made plans for their future. Years earlier at the height of their conflict, Mom filed for divorce, and Dad asked for a reconciliation, but that time it was met with demands and resentment. This time was different. They had lost their oldest daughter and seemed broken, and maybe they needed each other more than either of them wanted to admit.

"Dad and I are even getting sexy again," she told me with a giggle as the three of us sat at their kitchen table one afternoon.

I shot a look at Dad as he squirmed as though wanting to crawl under the table.

Wanting to save him from embarrassment, I said, "I won't tell you about my sex life if you don't tell me about yours."

"Great idea!" he exclaimed, relieved to have the topic brought to an end.

It was the first time in many years that I saw even a hint of contentment between my parents. They tried not to allow the scars that had formed in their hearts to define their new relationship. And although Mom's drinking didn't slow down, I figured that Dad was less miserable with a drunk wife than with no wife at all.

That July, Mom and Dad had just returned from vacationing in New England when he had undergone a routine physical that revealed a problem that required further testing. Since there was no longer a reason to worry about what was going on at home, I hadn't paid much attention to it. He was in the hospital for the testing, and I drove Mom to see him one afternoon. On the way home, I began to speak.

"I'm so happy that you and Dad are together again. With Liz being gone, you guys really need each other. I don't want to see either of you alone."

She said nothing but began to cry. I looked at her and saw agonizing, gripping pain in her face. I reached over and placed my hand on hers. The pain that registered on her face made me wince. I regretted bringing up Liz. It would have been better left unsaid, I thought.

She insisted I come in when we arrived at her house. I sat down at the kitchen table while she poured herself a drink.

It was early for drinking, but not too early for her. She offered to make me one, too.

"No thanks," I said.

She insisted.

"No, really, Mom, I don't want one."

She insisted again, this time with an edge in her voice. I let her make one for me.

I played with the rum, stirring the ice in the glass, while she sat down. She reached over and took my hand.

"Sue, Dad is sick. They found a tumor."

Tears welled up in the corners of my eyes. *God no*, I thought.

She told me the biopsy showed cancer, and that we would work together to get him well, that we'd get healthy as a family, that we'd stop eating bacon and butter, that his time working in the asbestos plant might have caused it, that he'd start chemo. That we'd pull through. These words seemed to bounce off my ears without registering, like a voice shouting into outer space. Mom kept talking, but I could no longer hear her.

It was then that I understood what her tears in the car were really about. They fell for her lost daughter, for her fractured marriage, for her uncertain future, for her husband who she decided after twenty-eight years she really did love after all. And for her unimaginable fear of losing him too.

My next visit to the hospital was scary and awkward. This time I went alone, and as I sat in Dad's room looking at him sitting up in his bed, the only words I could find were, "Mom told me, you know, about what's going on."

"Yeah," he said, with his gaze downcast.

There was no more to say.

My father's vulnerability revealed itself for the first time in that quiet hospital room. I felt uncomfortable at the awkwardness of the moment but remained there, sitting in my chair at the foot of his bed. Neither of us spoke for a long while.

A Bend in the Soul

Give sorrow words; the grief that does not speak knits
up the o-er wrought heart and bids it break.

—Shakespeare

It was December 2 that same year. Mom was preparing for Christmas, her favorite holiday. She loved to give gifts, and this year, her special gift was a marionette puppet she was making for Walter's daughter. I went home for Sunday breakfast that morning, and when it was time to leave, I paused in front of her, wrapped my arms around her, and said, "I love you, Mom."

"I love you too," she said. But she didn't look at me. There was a sadness in her face, and her emotions were not reflected in her words. They just sounded like, well, words. I suspected that this Christmas, the second one without Liz, was still difficult and she was further weighed down with worry about Dad. I promised myself I'd spend more time with her during the month.

The next evening, Walter and I were in the kitchen preparing dinner when the phone rang. I picked it up after the first ring.

"Sue?" It was my father.

"Hi, Dad!"

My father never called me. Maybe he was reaching out now that he was sick, I thought. We both were still making up for the years lost between us.

"Mom was choking. They took her to the hospital. Joey and I are leaving now."

"I'm coming!" I cried. I don't remember hanging up as Walter hurriedly reached to turn the stove off, leaving the half-cooked chicken breasts to gel in the pan. We ran out of the house. *This can't be happening*, I thought. I felt dazed as I tried to keep my senses intact. *She'll be fine*, I silently repeated. *They're just treating her.* The three-mile drive to the hospital seemed a lot longer.

As we stood nervously in the emergency room waiting area, Pat, my mother's friend, came running through the doors. Someone must have called her. She had been crying. Together, Dad, Joey, Walter, Pat, and I waited. For a very long time.

I wondered what was taking so long, considering that the doctors were merely clearing her airway. After what seemed like hours, a doctor approached and ushered us to a small room. We stood around him in a semicircle as he explained that Mom's heart had stopped. Massive coronary. Cardiac arrest. Died in the ambulance. Resuscitated. Pacemaker needed. These were words that I didn't expect to hear. They echoed in my head, and I reached for something to grab onto. The blood drained from my face as I felt my breath seize.

"We'll keep her here until we can get her stable," he said.

With that reassurance, there was nothing more we could do, so one by one, we walked out into the darkness and through the parking lot.

I drove back to my parents' house alone in stunned silence. I walked into the kitchen and found the table and chairs pushed to the side, and in my mind's eye saw the paramedics on their knees trying to resuscitate Mom. I saw a pool of vomit on the floor where she collapsed. Dropping to my knees, I cried.

The phone rang early the next morning. Dad was calling from the hospital.

"Sue, Mom's not doing very well. Dr. Cook is here, and you should come down."

Dr. Cook had been our family physician for more than twenty years.

A sane person would have dropped everything and raced to the hospital in that moment, but maybe Dad's words hadn't registered. I crawled out of bed and into the shower. I took the time to wash and style my hair, apply makeup, and choose something to wear. Looking back, my behavior seemed ghastly. But at the time, I didn't give it a second thought. Maybe I simply numbed out.

I arrived to find Dad and Dr. Cook standing outside Mom's ICU room. Dr. Cook began speaking.

"She isn't responding to any of the interventions. She's had over a hundred electroshocks. Her body rejected the pacemaker. There's not much more anyone can do. We can keep her going with machines, but she'll probably remain in a vegetative state. I'm afraid you need to decide."

What do you do when you are twenty-one years old and tasked with a decision like that? I desperately needed my mom, but for all intents and purposes, she was no longer there. Together with heaviness of heart that in that moment pulled the very life out of me, I agreed with my dad to let her go.

Dad held onto me as he walked me into her room. She lay on her back, bare-breasted with a sheet covering up to her belly. The quiet hum of a respirator sounded as my eyes followed the hose that extended out of it and attached to a mask that covered Mom's face. A nurse was performing chest compressions with no urgency. I stood looking down at her, angry that they allowed her to be so literally naked. *Why do they leave her exposed?* I thought. My mother was a modest woman, and her nakedness was an affront to me. After a moment, we left the room. We were not to be present when the machines were turned off. Only a few minutes had passed when Dr. Cook came out of the room.

"She's gone," she said.

Mom was forty-eight years old and not yet done raising her children.

The now insignificant fact that my parents hated each other for much of their twenty-eight-year marriage didn't seem to matter anymore. That morning was the only time I ever saw my father cry. We stood in the deserted hallway with the shiny tile floor and the distant sounds of doctors being summoned through the speakers in the ceiling, and we held onto each other.

Dr. Cook quietly uttered, "She's too young."

I didn't think so. The beauty Mom may have had in her younger years had been washed away by her grief of two lost children, years of depression, and an overflowing supply of hard liquor. I now believe that what set her final fate in motion was the choking death of my sister sixteen months earlier.

Dad and I walked out of the hospital into the cold December air. Another first was to see my father accept the offer of sedatives, so he took the prescription Dr. Cook gave him and went straight to the pharmacy as I drove alone back to their house. When I walked into the house, I closed the door behind me, fell against it, and screamed out a visceral pain that split my heart open.

Joey was given the news when he came home from high school later that day. He was barely in the door when Dad sat him down. "Mom died this morning," is all I remember him uttering in an uncomfortable softness that was out of character for him. Joey paused, said nothing, and climbed the stairs to his room and closed the door. I wondered what he was thinking. He wasn't close to Mom, but I couldn't imagine how he was processing this, if at all.

I learned from a neighbor who was a paramedic—and the first one on the scene the previous night—that Joey was in the living room when he heard a crash in the kitchen. Mom had been sitting in her favorite chair at the kitchen table near the window that looked out at the river and field behind our house, reading *Eye of the Needle*, smoking Salem cigarettes, and nursing one of her many cocktails she would drink that night, when she lunged forward and collapsed on the floor. Hearing the commotion, Joey ran in from the other room. He saw vomit on the floor next to her and thought she was choking. He got behind her, dropped to his knees, and tried to wrap his arms around her torso to perform the Heimlich, but her frame was too large for his fifteen-year-old body to maneuver. He frantically dialed 911.

Witnessing the death of two family members while he was so young had to leave inconceivable scars upon my brother's heart. When he finally emerged from his room later that evening, his eyes were swollen and red. It would be years before he ever mentioned our mother again.

A New Trajectory

Tears from the depths of some divine despair
Rise in the heart, and gather to the eyes,
In looking on the happy autumn fields,
And thinking of the days that are no more.

—Alfred Tennyson

I knew Dad was sick, but the depth of his illness was not shared with Joey. They had adored each other, and in the aftermath of Mom's death, I decided that my kid brother didn't need to fear what may never happen, so I avoided discussing anything to do with cancer while in his presence. Dad was Joey's hero, his best friend. He was always present at Joey's Indian Guides meetings. Indian Guides were like cub scouts, and it was a shared activity over which they bonded. Dad called him "Little José." To Joey, losing Dad was unthinkable.

In the weeks that followed Mom's death, and in spite of the hope I still held onto, I watched my father grow weaker. His weight continued to drop as the cancer and chemo continued to destroy his body. We took him out for his birthday dinner, but he spent most of it vomiting in the bathroom. Table conversation was without words, only knowing glances at each other as we waited for him to finish purging his meal into the toilet. It was becoming clear that in the microscopic war between cancer cells and white blood cells, the cancer was winning. In fear and frustration, Joey and I bore witness to Dad's deteriorating health. I reluctantly decided something had to be said, so one quiet afternoon while Joey and I sat at the kitchen table, I reached out and took his hand.

"If anything happens to Dad, you and I will stick together."

His body deflated as he dropped his gaze and muttered, "Yeah."

There was nothing more to say.

Dad must have known the end was near. I was at the house one day while Joey was in school, and we were in the living room with the television chattering. He turned to me and calmly said, "When the time comes, I want it to be like it was with Mom." And just as calmly turned his attention back to the television.

My mother was cremated, and he wanted the same. Without having to hear himself say the words, he was asking that we handle his body in the same manner. What it must have felt like for a man as proud as my father to face his own end—and soon—I will never know.

I looked at him a long time before I could speak. "Okay" is all I said, feeling the dagger penetrate once again.

He took a cab to the hospital a month later, two months after Mom died, probably knowing it was a one-way trip. I packed a suitcase and moved back into their house to take care of Joey.

His doctor later told me that Dad knew he had no more than three months to live. Dad being Dad, he didn't share that with us. Joey and I visited regularly, made gifts for him, decorated his hospital room with photos, and made plans for him to come home. I still had hope that he would hang on a few more years and, with that hope, I arranged for a visiting nurse to take care of him at home so I could continue to work.

This would never happen.

The call came from a relative one Saturday morning in early May.

"Your dad's had enough. He asked to be taken off all medication, no more blood transfusions, no more chemo, and no more surgeries."

"You need to come to the hospital," I was told. I was incredulous.

"Is he going to die *today?*" My voice cracked at the last syllable.

"Come alone, and don't tell Joey," was the reply.

I hung up and rushed out the door, past my brother, who had clearly overheard the conversation. What he must have felt at the time, I can't even imagine. I threw a quick glance at him, sitting on the sofa, his body sunken, his eyes staring blankly at the floor. Unlike me, Joey never considered that Dad's cancer was terminal. He may have just been too young to comprehend what this ghastly disease could do to someone.

So the job of explaining to him that Dad didn't have long to live was now mine. With Mom gone, I was the closest thing to an available adult he had.

Late one night a couple of days after the Saturday morning phone call, I took Joey into the study. My heart was already breaking, and at twenty-one, I didn't have the life experience or wisdom to know exactly how to handle the moment. So I just started talking.

"You know Dad is very sick," I began.

He pretty much figured out the rest. After a few quiet minutes, he asked, "Is he gonna be alive for my birthday?" That was two weeks away. "I don't know, Joey," was all I could say. I had to be honest with him. No false hopes, no promises I knew couldn't be kept. I held on to him as he cried and cried. He was fifteen years old and soon to be orphaned. The mother who he knew never loved him was dead, and his only remaining lifeline would soon be gone as well.

The next several days transpired in slow motion. I made calls to the circle of friends my parents had and told them that if they wanted to see Dad, they needed to come now. The following week saw friends and coworkers circulating through his hospital room. People who had long drifted away returned, along with those friends who were more like family. Quiet conferences took place between my dad's brother, his doctor, and me.

"He'll eventually go into a coma. Then it won't be long after that."

"Is he in pain?"

"No," the doctor told us. The conviction in his voice allowed me to believe he was telling the truth.

I continued to go to work every day but left at noon to drive to the hospital, where I'd stay with him until late into the night. I sat on his bed, held his hand, talked to him. Sometimes we would just sit in each other's presence, saying nothing. When he was strong enough to sit up, I sat behind him on the bed and wrapped my arms around him. I'd tell him how much I loved him in some seemingly hopeless effort to make up for all of those lost years between us. I did love him, I always loved him, and he needed to hear it. Over and over, I said, "I love you, Dad. I love you, Dad. I love you, Dad."

Sunday, May 18, we were gathered outside his room. Joey, Uncle Warren, Aunt Lou from South Carolina, Walter, and me. The coma had arrived two days before. I'd never seen my father asleep before, so I was taken aback by the half-closed distant gaze in his eyes as he lay sleeping in the bed. The doctor was surprised that he was still hanging on and remarked about his strong heart.

"That's from years of running five miles a day," I said. I wanted to kick the cancer demons for invading my father's body when he had worked so hard to turn his health around.

Before the coma set in, I went jogging one evening to get some air, making a route around town and through the neighborhoods of Summit, passing the old colonial houses with large front yards, detached garages, and tall oak and maple trees. It was a beautiful backdrop to the ongoing heartbreak in room 805 at Overlook Hospital. I came back to Dad's room to tell him how far I ran. He was proud of me. I wanted him to be. I wanted him to know that I wanted to be like him. He was, after all the years I had denied it, a role model for me.

That Sunday evening, the nurses moved his roommate to another room so "family could have privacy." Later, Uncle Warren went home, and Aunt Lou took Joey back to the house, leaving Walter and me to stay by Dad's side. By this time, I had not left the hospital for several days and had turned the waiting room down the hall into a makeshift bedroom. Walter and I sat with him, each of us in our own chairs. Mine was at the foot of his bed. The room was empty except for the bed he was lying in, the myriad of cards and gifts displayed along the windowsill, the nurses' chart hanging on a clipboard on the wall, and a television that was broadcasting the eruption of Mount St. Helens. The only sounds in the room were Dad's own intermittent breathing and the humming of the air pump that kept his mattress inflated. I timed his breath. One every fifteen seconds. I wondered how he could breathe so slowly. The sound penetrated my brain with increasing volume, blocking out all thought. I sat at the foot of his bed with my head in my hands and started to cry. I said to Walter, "I don't want to lose him, but I can't stand seeing him this way!" I had repeated these words often throughout the last week, always in the hallway where Dad wouldn't see me crying.

"Come with me," Walter said. "You can't stay here."

He lifted me out of the chair and walked me to my room down the hall. I lay down on the vinyl sofa, fully clothed, and fell asleep before I knew where I was. My next memory seemed to come in an instant, like coming out of anesthesia and feeling like no time had passed. Walter was in the room, trying to wake me up. It was 3:15 a.m. He sat down across from me and said, "Sue, your father died."

"No! No!" I cried. My body froze, and my breath seized. The room spun into a vortex, sucking the last bit of air with it. The moment had come, and I didn't want to believe it. I wanted so badly to rewind the clock, if only to have a few more minutes to tell Dad how much I loved him one more time. Walter pulled me to my feet and held onto me as we walked down the hall to Dad's room. We passed a nurse leaving his room, and she was crying. The nurses loved Dad. He was always a gentleman, they said, all the way to the end.

His room was literally dead silent. The air pump turned off, his breathing stopped. I stood next to his bed and looked at him. I had never seen a dead person before. Even moments after the soul has left the body, a person's appearance changes. *Dead people don't look like they're sleeping*, I thought. *They look dead.* Their body becomes a shell, and it's obvious that something is missing. The life force that occupied it is gone. I imagined his soul was still hovering above near the ceiling, and I wanted to look up, but I was afraid. I just stared down at him. With nothing to say, I stood there, burning the image of my dead father into my brain. I never wanted to forget.

Walter and I drove back to his house in silence while the world slept. Exhausted and numb, we went to bed for a couple of hours and then drove to my parents' house. It was 7 a.m., and Aunt Lou was coming down the stairs as I walked through the front door.

"He's gone," I said.

She exhaled deeply and quietly asked, "What time?"

I told her a little after three that morning.

"I woke up then and was thinking of him," she said.

That's no coincidence, I thought. His soul came to say good-bye. I've heard of this type of thing happening—family members wake up at the moment a loved one passes somewhere else. It comforted me to think that my father's soul was somewhere nearby. Joey came downstairs a few minutes later, and I told him. His face wore a resignation that said he had already reconciled this in his mind.

My kid brother was now an orphan.

Later that day, we began the now familiar task of making phone calls, meeting with the funeral director, and ordering flowers. There is a ritual involved in burying a dead person. Maybe it's so the bereaved are forced to stay focused. Maybe it's to give us something to do. Maybe it's so we don't crumble. Either way, we have to get out of bed and walk to the bathroom. We have to go to the kitchen. We have to make the breakfast. We have to breathe in. We have to breathe out.

During this process, my body stayed in motion, but my heart closed. I remember the funeral. I remember behaving like life was normal, smiling and chatting with people. I remember not remembering why I was there. I acted more like a hostess than a grieving daughter, unaware of the whispers and glances from my parents' friends. I greeted people with the demeanor of a Stepford Wife: a polished outward appearance, but a heart and soul devoid of all emotion. I sat legs crossed and well composed in my snug knee-length skirt and neatly pressed scoop-neck summer blouse as the minister stood at the podium and offered his scripted words of wisdom and condolence. Eyeing my chin-length hair perfectly styled and tucked behind my ears, no one would have guessed that I was burying the third member of my family in less than two years. It was only when the minister mentioned this monumental detail that I felt myself flinch. That rocked me. That stole my breath. That's when I crumbled, and that's when my life's trajectory shifted again.

The Promised Land

In this house of clay and water, my heart lies in ruin without you.
Dear Soul, please enter this house, so I can begin to rebuild.

—Rumi

In the weeks that followed my father's death, the feeling of needing to run began to again stir inside me. Joey's sixteenth birthday came and went, but I didn't remember much of it. I think Uncle Warren came by, and I think somebody called on the phone. Time somehow swept over that day and the days that followed, taking all memory with it. I was in survival mode, and in order to survive, I had to run.

By the end of June, I was granted a leave of absence from my secretarial job. I still wasn't sure what I would do or where I would go, but I *was* going. I had to get out. California always had a certain appeal to me, ever since I was twelve years old when I learned that my heartthrob, David Cassidy, lived there. I grew up and out of my crush, but I still felt a draw to the land that was far enough away to help me forget.

I arranged for Joey to stay with my parents' best friends, and on July 1, I said good-bye to Walter and boarded a plane for San Francisco with an open-return ticket in my hand. When I would come home, I didn't know nor did I care.

Being summer in San Francisco, it was cold and foggy. It's said that the Bay Area has four seasons: winter, spring, winter, fall. I wasn't prepared for the wet chill in the air as I walked out of the airport and climbed into a taxi. I found a little hotel downtown that had an old-fashioned elevator, the kind with the accordion gate that pulled closed and required the rider to stand patiently as it moved slowly between floors. Although crawling backward up the stairs on hands and knees would have gotten me there faster, it didn't matter; I wasn't in a hurry to go anywhere. I had no plans, no agenda, and no desire to ever go back home. My only plan was to start walking and see where my feet led me.

At the corner of Hyde and Lombard, I climbed onto a stone wall to get a better view across the city landscape. In the distance to the east, beyond the descending zigzag of Lombard Street, was Coit Tower. I clicked off a few frames with my Minolta when I heard someone behind me say, "Hi there! Taking pictures?" I looked down to see someone looking up at me, and I climbed down to street level to find myself face-to-face with a good-looking, bright-eyed young man with an ear-to-ear smile.

"I'm Gregg," he said, still smiling as though his face was frozen that way. "These are my friends," he added as he gestured to a car that was idling at the corner. There were three other young, bright-eyed, smiling people in it. I saw the driver, whose name was Hank, his passenger, and another person in the backseat. Gregg and I walked over to their car and began chatting. I told them I'd just arrived from New Jersey. No, I didn't know how long I was staying. No, I didn't have any plans. No, I didn't know where I was going after this.

"We're hosting a dinner tonight at our place. Why don't you join us?" They seemed friendly enough, and I really didn't have any reason to say no, so I agreed. Besides, it was an opportunity for another adventure, and I was all in. Gregg opened the back door of the car and gestured for me to get in. He was still smiling. What a lucky break, I thought. Landing in a distant city, far from home, and making friends the first day! I was going to like this.

My new friends' house on Bush Street seemed dark, even though the lights were on and it was still daylight. It was an older building with wide hallways, ornate trim, and dark wood railings. The furniture was dated and nondescript. There were a few other people mingling about, picking at the food that was laid out on a table in the hallway. After a short time of small talk, we were ushered into what looked like the living room to hear a man named Noah speak.

Noah seemed to be the person in charge that evening. He was a thin man of average height with large eyeglasses and a comb-over that didn't quite hide his almost completely receded hairline. He spoke softly but did a good job of engaging everyone's attention. His lecture was about God and the church and things of that nature that I had no interest in hearing. I was more interested in being with other young people who, like me, seemed to be on a journey in their lives.

We were told that "the Family" (as they called themselves) had a camp north of the city, and we were all invited there. We could live there for a while and work on the farm and learn more about the future of our world. There was a bus leaving that night that could take us there. I was intrigued. I wanted to go, but not until I had more time to explore the city. I'd catch another bus in a couple of days.

"There's no other bus," a girl named Becky told me. Becky had been in the car with Gregg and the others. "There's only one, and it's leaving tonight." I thought about it for a minute and, not wanting to miss an opportunity for adventure, decided to give up the hotel room I'd already paid for and go along with the group.

Becky offered to come with me back to my hotel and pack up my things. If it seemed at all unusual that these people—strangers, really—were going out of their way to stay with me, it didn't occur to me at the time. I just saw them as new friends. We gathered my belongings into two suitcases—one with clothes and the other with a sleeping bag and camping gear—and returned to the house on Bush Street in time to load the bus. By now, it was late in the evening, and the sun had long disappeared below the horizon, so my normally good sense of direction was thrown off. I only knew we were heading north because we crossed the Golden Gate Bridge. I looked out my window at the enormous steel and cables that ascended into the night sky and thought it was the most majestic thing I'd ever seen. Soon after, I was asleep.

Two hours later, the bus full of sleepy travelers pulled through the gates of a farm in Boonville. We were ushered off the bus and into the building to spread out sleeping bags and blankets and drop back into sleep. Gregg stayed close by, and I welcomed the comfort that only a big brother could offer. That night, I had a vivid dream. I walked into my father's hospital room moments after he died to see him being encased in a large plastic bag. He suddenly sat up in his bed and opened his eyes. He looked around with a dazed expression, and I began screaming, "He's not dead!" I ran down the hall to tell the nurses that he was still alive, but they wouldn't or couldn't hear me. They rolled him out of the room and down the hall into a void. I woke up in tears and sweat. The next night I had the same dream. The following night, I dreamt about my mother, that she wasn't dead either. I told Gregg about the nightmares, and he said that I should line my sleeping bag with garlic to ward off any more bad dreams.

In spite of my nightmares, I was quickly growing fond of my new surroundings. Boonville was spread out in a valley cradled among rolling hills the color of roasted sesame seeds and a few lone Wilderness Oak trees accentuating the landscape in the distance. Each day began at sunrise, followed by prayer, a breakfast of pancakes, toast, lots of carbohydrates, singing, and a lecture or two. Lectures were always classroom-style, and topics were limited to the church and the Family, with passages from the Bible woven in to allow the message to make sense. I never read the Bible as a child, so I took it all at face value. Occasionally, someone would ask a question, and the reply was invariably, "You'll learn about it in the next lecture." Hard, direct questions were never answered, but I paid little attention to the whole matter because I loved my new community. My family of origin—the one that was now mostly gone—was fractured, damaged, and mostly emotionally absent while I was growing up, and the people I was with now filled the void that remained. The sense of love and friendship I felt at Boonville was in stark contrast to the growing loneliness I'd left behind in New Jersey.

I was never alone, except for in the shower. Gregg became my constant companion and was always close by. I learned that he was from upstate New York, that he was a year or two older than me, that his parents were initially unhappy with his choice to join the Family but later accepted it. We shared a lot with each other, and I felt safe with him. He truly was becoming my big brother.

In the afternoon of the first day at the farm, our task was to harvest the garlic in the fields. About fifteen people—including Gregg and me—worked to yield a crop of hundreds of heads. Some of us pulled the garlic from the ground, some tilled the soil, some braided the leaves from each stalk, and each person was given the opportunity to sing. Singing was a big thing on the farm. A songbook was passed around as we worked. I kept my head down in hopes I wouldn't be noticed. I still was having panic attacks, and any spotlight that was on me usually triggered one. So singing in public, or even speaking in public, was something

I desperately avoided. Ultimately, the book was handed to me and I couldn't hide anymore. I had been holding my breath out of fear, and when I had no choice but to reach out and take it, I felt my body deflate. With a lump in my throat and a rock in my stomach, I slowly put the shovel down and flipped through the book. I landed on the song "You Are My Sunshine," took a deep breath, and sang it with a trembling voice, out of key and very quickly, and in the end, was met with an explosion of cheers and applause. It didn't matter that my voice shook or that I sang out of tune. These people loved me.

I was finally home.

I had never before experienced this sense of togetherness and community. The years of discord I lived with growing up was what I believed to be normal. Didn't all parents fight like mine did? Didn't all parents drink like mine did? And didn't all parents beat each other on Christmas Eve like mine did?

My time at Boonville drafted a different narrative of what family could be. It didn't matter that life on the farm was hard. And it *was* hard. We worked all the time, but when we weren't cooking for the hundred or so people who lived there or cleaning up after them or working in the fields or sitting for hours listening to lectures, we were square-dancing on a hilltop at sunset or swimming in a watering hole with our clothes on. I was falling in love with my new life.

Around the seventh day, we were told it was time to move on. (Move on *where?*) Another bus would take us to our next location near Santa Rosa. The bus pulled into Boonville late that night, and we piled on with our belongings. It never occurred to me why we were leaving or why we only traveled at night. It just seemed to be the way things were done, no questions asked, no information offered.

I slept during the drive and woke up as our bus crossed the bridge over a stream and entered through the gates at Camp K sometime in the night. I stumbled out, half asleep, and wandered into a cabin with my sleeping bag and knapsack. Gregg was with me, as was Becky and a few other new friends from Boonville, although women and men were assigned separate sleeping quarters. In the morning, I woke to the smell of crisp northern California air. This place was even more beautiful than the farm. The clean air turned the sky a Persian blue, and the evergreens were soaked in shades of emerald, olive, and moss. I had never been in such a beautiful place.

I was at Camp K for a few days when I fell very ill. I lay on the floor of the girls' cabin in my sleeping bag, hot with fever and struggling to breathe. My body ached from head to toe, and a river of phlegm flowed through my windpipe. There was no medicine at the camp, so the remedy was hot tea and serenade. Becky, Gregg, Hank, and several others I didn't know stood around me as my limp body lay on the floor, barely aware of their presence. They sang *"We love you Su-ooo, oh yes we do-oo … we don't love anyone … as much as you-uu. When you're not with us, we're blue! Oh Sue-oo we love you, yes we doooooo!"*

I was loved. And as bad as I felt, it was all I needed. I drifted off to sleep with a hint of warmth in my heart.

I was happy to see that Noah was also at the camp. There was nothing overtly attractive about him, but I found myself being drawn to him anyway. Maybe it was the authority-figure thing, or maybe it was his geekiness I found so appealing. In any event, I began finding reasons to be near him. I sat next to him during meals and forced myself out of bed before fully recovering from the flu just to play dodgeball, knowing he would be playing. "You're so righteous," he said to me. If only he knew.

I felt like a teenager again, wanting to be kept in the protective fold of a man's heart. I became obsessive, never wanting to be far from him. I made sure I was placed in his group or in the front of the room during his lectures. I kept watch for him as I walked from my cabin to the main building, from the dodgeball field to the lecture hall. My heart danced a little jig whenever I caught sight of him. If he went back to the city, I wanted to know when he would be returning.

One afternoon, I asked Noah if we could talk. He never gave me reason to think he had any interest in me, and my unrequited affection was beginning to cause me pain. I needed to let him know just how I felt, hoping this disclosure would put me on his emotional radar.

We sat on a wooden bench outside a cabin, the summer air warm and dry. Instead of opening my heart and allowing him the chance to respond, I spoke through the lump in my throat as I abruptly said, "I've decided to leave. I'm falling in love with you, Noah, and it's hurting too much."

"You can't leave," he said. "I've given my heart to you." I stared back at him, not expecting to hear this. He was looking right at me, but his eyes were blank and his words lacked inflection. I knew in my heart that he was lying. I wanted to believe him, I wanted him to convince me that he really *did* give his heart to me, but the feeling in my gut revealed more truth than his words ever could. Still, I allowed myself to believe his lie. And I stayed.

At the camp, we were encouraged to share. I mean, to share about ourselves openly to the group and privately to another person, usually someone with seniority. I talked a lot with Gregg and Becky, my "spiritual parents," as they were called. I shared about my sister and parents' deaths and about other mistakes I made in my life. I shared about the small trust fund my father had left Joey and me. These were like mini therapy sessions. I talked and cried and let the grief wash through me, knowing I could trust my new family, which was how they were beginning to feel to me. I gave them my heart, knowing they would hold it safely in their hands. Of course, I assumed that what I spoke of would remain confidential. So I was curious how the lecture later that afternoon was about the spirits of our deceased parents guiding us to the Family. This got my attention, and I wondered how much truth there was to it. The timing of that particular message relative to my sharing earlier in the day did seem a little more than interesting, but I chose to ignore the coincidence. The other new recruits also had questions, but we were always told to "wait until the next lecture."

Over time, I traded in my lingering doubts for the unspoken promise of a new life, in a new place, with a new family. I felt so bonded to my friends that I was willing to believe anything I was told. I swallowed it all because the risk of losing them was too great by now.

We all had jobs at the camp. Sometimes we helped prepare meals, and other times we were assigned cleanup duty. Some people handled the laundry, which involved driving into town. None of the new people were assigned that task; we didn't leave the camp. When I went jogging in the morning, it was on the road outside the gate, so Gregg and at least one other person always went with me. I thought it a bit odd that Gregg jogged in a dress shirt, slacks, and street shoes. I was still curious, but not enough that I bothered to ask about it.

Washing pots and pans after dinner was a tedious task, so we oftentimes sang to alleviate boredom. One evening after dinner while cleaning up with Gregg and a couple of other people, we began to sing. Like at the farm, Camp K always had voices ringing out somewhere. The songs were very random and not of any particular selection. "Swing Low, Sweet Chariot" made its way into our medley, and each of us took turns making up a verse. By then, I was used to singing in front of the group, and I belted out lyrics that seemed to effortlessly form in my head. We broke into laughter, and my heart literally soared. *God, I love this.*

One of the jobs assigned to me was to help build a tree house. Gregg acted as foreman, and we got busy hauling lumber, nails, saws, and paint. The tree selected was along the main path leading halfway up the hill to the dodgeball field, past cabins, showers, and offices where the camp personnel worked. The tree itself had large, low-lying branches that made it perfect for climbing. With four or five of us working, it took no more than four days to build. When we were done, we stood back and admired our beautiful structure. It was at least one hundred square feet and had enough room to host a small group. All it needed was paint.

"Go on down to the guard house," Gregg said to me. "They have a can of red paint."

The guard house, which was always occupied, was at the entrance to the camp at the bottom of the hill, just inside the gates that remained closed. As I walked down the hill, I was probably fifty feet away when I saw someone familiar standing on the other side of the gate. I slowed down and then stopped. It was Walter. *What the hell?* At first it felt like I was stepping into a dream before it sank in that he was actually there. It didn't make sense. I was so far away and hadn't spoken to him in days. He had sent several letters to me telling me how much he missed me, but never did I think he would actually show up. And since I didn't know where I was, how could he? The only address either of us had was a post office box in Santa Rosa. I slowly kept walking toward the gate. I would be lying to say I was happy to see him. But what could I do? He had already spotted me.

I approached him, both of us on either side of the gate. He reached out to put his arms around me, and I allowed myself to be pulled toward him, my body rigid and devoid of any genuine warmth. He held on tight, and after an uncomfortable amount of time, I pulled away. By now, Gregg and Gemma (a Family senior) were there, and they were clearly concerned about this new development.

"Do you want to go for a ride? Get something to eat?" Walter asked. I didn't want to go, and I said as much. He tried for several minutes to convince me to go with him, even going so far as to imply he had cancer and needed me with him. Even though my heart was with my new family at Camp K, I still felt an obligation to Walter. Before I could reply, Gemma stepped in, clearly on the verge of panic.

"You can't go with him, Sue. If you do, you'll lose all your spirituality!" What came out of my mouth next surprised even me.

"That's ridiculous, Gemma, God is with me wherever I go!"

"No, Sue! Families always come and take people away! They lock them in a room and won't let them out!"

I had never heard of anything so outrageous, and by now I was getting angry. Why were they so hell-bent on keeping me there? My need to prove her wrong trumped my desire to stay. Right then, I turned and walked out the gate toward the car. Turning around, I said, "I'll come back, I swear I will!" I slid into the backseat, and Walter got in next to me.

Walter's friend Chris was behind the wheel, and Walter and I were in the backseat. I was still too preoccupied with Gemma's remarks to bother asking why Chris was there in the first place.

Chris seemed to be driving fast while navigating turns in the Sonoma County country roads, all of which were windy with very little shoulder. A few minutes down the road, he slammed the brakes and turned the wheel, making a sudden and violent U-turn that made the car rock back and forth, then another one so we were facing ahead again. The car screeched to a stop as dust began to rise from the road. Walter reached past me, threw the door open, and pushed me out. Bewildered, I looked around and saw another car pull up from nowhere behind us. I looked at the driver; it was Uncle Warren. *What the hell was going on?*

Instinctively, I turned to run, but Walter grabbed me, dragged me into the second car, threw me into the backseat and held me down on the floor. The sounds of my screaming drowned out the shouting, the tires skidding, the gravel flying, and the roar of the engine as both cars raced away.

Walter released his grip when I finally stopped struggling. I slowly crawled onto the seat and sat up, stunned. The question of what was happening could not even form in my mind yet. No one spoke as the car glided along the road on a mission to get out of the area. Uncle Warren and the man sitting next to him stared straight ahead at the road without uttering a sound.

For more than an hour, I had no idea what direction we were traveling. My usual accurate sense of direction was turned around by the night driving from farm to camp. Then I saw the Golden Gate Bridge up ahead and realized that we'd soon be back in the city. The car would have to stop eventually, and that's when I would have a chance to run. As we inched our way through traffic, we slowly passed Bush Street, near where I had been at the house that first night. I inched closer to the door, but Walter reached over and tightly wrapped his arms around me. There was no way I'd be able to get out of the car.

We crossed the bridge into Oakland and turned south onto the 880. I carefully kept an eye on where we were going so I'd know how to get back to the house on Bush Street. If I could make it that far, I could get word to Noah or Gregg and they'd have someone pick me up and bring me back to my new family at Camp K.

The car eventually turned into a driveway in front of a townhouse. Two other cars pulled in next to us. I sat staring ahead as car doors started opening and people cautiously emerged like bears from winter hibernation. I opened my door, glanced around, and nonchalantly started to walk toward the street. I didn't get to the end of the driveway before someone they referred to as "security" stopped me. A tall man-boy, looking no older than twenty-two, stepped into my path and made it very clear that he wasn't going to let me go any farther.

My head was spinning but all I knew was that I was somewhere in the East Bay. I was quickly escorted into the townhouse to a bedroom on the second floor.

Gemma was right. I *was* locked in a room. The worst part was I didn't have any understanding of what was happening, who these people were that had followed in other cars, why they were there, or when I would be allowed to leave.

The next several days moved along with an awareness of being nowhere, in no time, with strangers among me. Confused and shaken, I was desperate to get away. But like my time with the Family, I was never left alone. Someone was always in the room with me. The hours and minutes dripped from the clock as I lay on the bed, sleeping or staring at the ceiling or at the walls or at the darkness under the covers, while the strangers among me filtered in and out of the room. The older man who had been in the car with Uncle Warren knelt down next to my bed and began reading something aloud out of a book, but my mind didn't register the words. My most vivid memory was of a book that sat on a table next to the bed. It was about Lorne Michaels and the creation of *Saturday Night Live*. I lay on my side, eyes transfixed on the book's cover. When I got bored, I stared at the spine, following the contours of the book with my eyes. My back was to the room so I wouldn't have to acknowledge whoever was there. Once I glanced over my shoulder to see man-boy sitting on the floor, his knees up and his forearms resting on them. He looked at me, and I turned away.

My waking hours were consumed with desperation to get back to the camp in the hills and the people I loved. I wondered if my new family was looking for me. I was frantic to get a message to them. I felt trapped. There was no escape; I couldn't even be in the bathroom by myself. These people were telling me that my new family was fake, that they wanted to hurt me and keep me from my real family. (*What* family? The ones who were already *dead?*) They told me the group who called themselves "The Family" was really the Unification Church and that they were a cult. This meant nothing to me, and even if they were a cult, I didn't care. I had to get back to them. The message my captors were giving me was that the wizard hiding behind this curtain was evil. Confusion, anger, and despondency were my new companions.

Eventually, after what I guessed was several days and with no apparent way out, I gave in. Whatever these people wanted—Uncle Warren, Walter, Chris, the others—they could have it. I'd stopped eating the day I arrived in protest of my captivity, so asking for a cheeseburger must have somehow made them feel victorious and suggested a breakthrough of sorts. I was then allowed to leave my room and was invited to join the group downstairs, where they gathered for meals. Conversation flowed among them as I sat, numb and heartbroken. My heart felt heavier than it had ever been as I realized then that I would not return to Santa Rosa and the life and people I loved.

"I'd like to take her to Tucson," I heard the older man say. "I think we could help her there." The older man seemed to be the one in charge, so the next day after Chris and Uncle Warren left to fly back to New Jersey, he and young man-boy, Walter, and I began the drive south to Tucson, where I lived for the next several weeks with the older man and his wife.

False Prophet

There is a voice that doesn't use words. Listen.

—Rumi

As time passed in Tucson, I began to accept my situation. I still longed for my Santa Rosa life, but my hosts were very kind and I couldn't ignore the sense that they only wanted to help me. Their names were Joe and Esther, and they were the same age my parents would have been. I couldn't ignore the fact that they hardly knew me, yet they opened their home to me and made me feel welcome. I swam in their pool and ate meals with them. We spent evenings in their hot tub and hours talking at the kitchen table. They shared about their lives in Ohio before moving out west. They married young, and soon after started their family, raising five children, one of whom would go on to do his father's work of "rescuing" people. They were simple people. Esther spoke with a quiet southern Ohio twang; Joe was a World War II veteran with eyes that exposed a personal pain he chose not to talk about. Even his smile revealed a certain sadness. And yet, all they did was love me. Although I could come and go freely, no longer confined to a room with a constant shadow behind me, I felt an invisible tether that tugged at my conscience telling me I should stay with them.

Joe and Esther explained to me about the Unification Church, the Moonies. I learned they practiced mind control, or brainwashing, on people. Many of whom, like me, were young and starry-eyed, recruited off city streets. I was being "indoctrinated" into the cult and would eventually, Joe and Esther said, lose all free will and ability to think for myself. My life would be completely in the hands of the Moonies. I was told they would eventually convince me to quit my job, sign over the small trust fund my parents left me, and cut off ties to everyone I knew.

"They'd put you with the congressmen," Esther said. She believed I'd be used as a prostitute of sorts for politicians who came to town.

"That's what they do with the young pretty girls," she added.

I spent as much time alone as I could, trying to make sense of what I was being told. I had a deep longing for Noah, Gregg, Hank, Collette, and the tight community to which I felt a part. They had become my new family, and I had a new home. And now I was being told none of it was real.

Was it all a lie?

My heart was broken, and I tried to reconcile my deep feelings of love and belonging to the Family—as I still insisted on calling them—against a profile of deceit and manipulation I was now being told was at the heart of the organization. It all seemed outrageous.

In spite of this, I still longed for my Santa Rosa life. I thought that if I could make my way back, none of what I learned about the group would matter, or even happen, and I could resume my wonderful life with the people I loved in the beautiful hills of northern California. My heart was in a tug-of-war, and in a moment of weakness, Santa Rosa won out. I made a plan to run.

The bedroom where I slept was at the opposite end of the house from the garage. I knew where the car keys were kept in the kitchen and would wait until everyone was asleep and tiptoe out of the house. I'd push the car out of the carport and into the street, roll it down the hill, start the engine, and be gone. It would be morning before anyone noticed, and by then I'd be over the state line back in California, headed north. It was perfect. I can do this, I said to myself. I thought back to a time in my adolescence when I climbed out of my second-floor bedroom window late one night, falling into the arms of my friends waiting below. Mom had talked me into the idea that Dad had a gun and was unstable so I'd better get away. I only half believed her but took the bait because I loved an adventure, any kind of adventure.

Later that night in Tucson, I lay in bed and stared into the darkness. And waited. The house grew quiet, and soon it would be time to go. I rehearsed my exit over and over in my head. Go quietly, slip out, be gone. I needed to go soon or I'd miss my window. *Come on!* I thought. *Go! Go now!*

But I couldn't do it. Joe and Esther's faces stared back at me in the darkness of my mind and the quiet of my room. Leaving like that would devastate them, not because they'd see it as a personal failure, but because I truly believed they loved me like their own daughter. And my affection for them was growing stronger as well.

As desperately as I wanted to leave that night, guilt held me back. I hated my conscience because the decision to follow it or not would define how I would see myself from that moment on. I literally gripped the sides of the bed until I fell asleep. When morning broke, I let go of any thought of running.

Walter had stayed with me in Tucson. I didn't want him there but accepted his presence as an unwelcome accessory. The Family taught us about God love and pure love, and the daily lectures delivered an undercurrent message of chastity. I didn't completely swallow it at the time, and on occasion would argue with Noah or anyone else who would engage in such a conversation about the virtue of a healthy sex life. But because I was taken away so violently and reacted by hanging on to anything the Family espoused, I refused Walter's advances.

And there were many. Sometimes he lay in bed next to me, and I'd recoil when I felt his hand on me. In truth, he repulsed me. I was still angry that he showed up at the gate at Camp K uninvited, that he threw me into a car, that he was the one who orchestrated my abduction. Or maybe I was disgusted by my own behavior and how I allowed myself to get into this situation, and he happened to be the object of that disgust.

Maybe I objectified him as the revulsion toward myself and toward my selfish behavior when my family was alive.

Maybe I always wanted to leave him. Maybe I had always been ashamed of bedding down with my high school teacher.

Maybe he was, in the final analysis, a painful reminder of the life I so badly wanted to leave behind.

Betrayed

We learned to ignore our inner voice because the people in our life who mattered to us did not listen to it. Because they treated our inner voice like it didn't matter, we came to believe that it didn't matter. So eventually, their voice became louder within us than our own voice.

—Teal Swan

Eventually, summer passed, and with the arrival of September, I decided I couldn't stay in Tucson any longer. I wondered what to do next, where to go. With a deep sadness and reluctance in my heart, I decided that the only place left to go was back to New Jersey. Joe and Esther drove Walter and me to the airport, and after exchanging hugs, tears, and promises, we boarded the plane.

As I stepped onto the tarmac at New York's Kennedy airport, I was slapped with a blast of late-summer humidity and the sobering thought that I had just returned to the home that wasn't home anymore. If I had felt lost the day I left New Jersey, I was now completely adrift. I couldn't see further than the next day.

Walter and I drove home to my parents' house, which by now had been reduced to a graveyard of bad memories. Joey's time staying with our parents' friends put a tremendous strain on all of them. He needed to live in the house that was familiar to him, and I needed to take care of him. At twenty-one years old and still devastated by all that had happened in the last nine months, I became the angry, grieving caretaker of my angry, grieving teenage brother.

I moved into Liz's room on the top floor and returned to work the following week. I could function enough to handle simple tasks but didn't have much left in the way of executive functioning or decision-making ability. I hadn't yet begun to process the summer, and the thought of having to do so wasn't even on my radar. Day-to-day survival was the most I could manage. Walter moved in as well, but I offered no objections because I simply didn't care.

As the days passed, a new, unfamiliar heaviness descended on me. The expanding hollowness was swallowing me whole. I forced myself to go through the motions of getting out of bed, going to work, bathing, and living. But something inside me was missing, like a full-color motion picture screen that faded to silent static. I was merely existing, nothing more. There was a darkness approaching that I'd never felt before.

Depression didn't come on suddenly. In fact, I didn't realize it was happening until I had fallen deeply into it. Like mind control, it crept in, little by little, without uttering its presence yet consuming all aspects of me.

By the time I realized what was happening, it was too late; I was buried under the weight of despair. There was an unconscious shift in perspective, a change in outlook. The things I once found pleasurable lost their appeal, and I didn't know why. My *joie de vivre* had long ago disappeared. I was trapped at the bottom tier of Maslow's hierarchy of needs: survival. It became harder to get out of bed. Food lost its taste. My once colorful world was reduced to shades of gray, which eventually faded into a blackness that, like a vortex, pulled me down, down, away from any sensation of what it felt like to be alive.

Pain and sadness wrapped themselves around my heart like a vice, and it hurt. Like trying to inhale with an elephant on my chest, the struggle to breath made me nauseous. My facial muscles couldn't form a smile. Anything that required interacting with the outside world was a struggle. I just wanted to not exist. Maybe that's why people commit suicide, I thought. Not to die, but because there seems no other way to make the pain stop. Even with my brother near me and a job I managed to go to most days, I felt surrounded by nothing but darkness.

One night, the phone rang. The call was from a physician who had heard about what happened in California. His son had also been involved in the same organization, and he wanted to help. He gave me the name of a psychiatrist who had worked with his son, and I wrote down the number, politely thanked him, and said good-bye. I didn't believe in psychiatry and initially dismissed the notion of calling him. My parents hadn't believed in psychiatry, and since I was, in part, a product of my upbringing, I felt there was something inherently wrong with paying money to a stranger to figure out my problems. But the depression was holding me hostage, and my options were running out. So several days later, I sequestered myself in a room with the door locked and dialed the number on the piece of paper.

His secretary put me on hold, and after a brief silence, he picked up the phone. I introduced myself and told him about the referral and gave him a brief summary of what had happened over the summer.

"Who do you live with?" His voice had a squeaky quality that was punctuated by a relaxed West Indian accent. When I explained that most of my family was dead and I was taking care of my teenage brother, he said, "Oh my, you need to see me." I saw a lifeline thrown toward me, and I reached out and grabbed it. I made an appointment for the following Tuesday.

I kept the appointment a secret. Ashamed and scared, I wasn't sure what to expect and had no reference for this type of thing. So I didn't tell anyone where I was going that afternoon.

I arrived at his office building on the campus in Newark and found a parking space inside the chain-link fenced parking lot. This section of town was particularly bad, and the fence provided a small barrier of safety. His office was located in a sanitary-blue one-story building that looked no different than the rows of identical buildings within the medical compound. I walked through the double doors down a concrete-lined hallway, turned left, down another hallway, and entered room 1501 on the right. A young heavy-set woman behind a desk greeted me and told me to have a seat. I nervously remained standing.

I glanced around the room, registering in my mind the typical accoutrements one would normally find in a psychiatrist's office. A secretary's desk, metal filing cabinet, piles of journals and books, a metal coat rack, and a collection of waiting room magazines that were as outdated as the furniture. I consider this room the buffer zone.

Relieved that I got myself this far but too nervous to sit, I lingered a few minutes more, standing. I noticed above the secretary's desk a newspaper clipping taped to the wall. It was an article and photo—I assumed it was him—about a local psychiatrist who went to South America to help the survivors of the Jonestown mass suicide two years before. The man in the photo was short, heavyset, and dark-skinned, with a comb-over that didn't quite hide his advanced receding hairline, and eyeglasses that gave him a bug-eyed appearance. Praise and reverence was the flavor of the article.

I turned my attention to the sound of a door opening, and in walked the man from the photo. His eyes were more piercing in person and I nervously offered my hand in response to the hand he extended to greet me. He led me into his office and I glanced around to take in the scene: a large room with a desk, shelves that barely held together the notebooks and papers thrown at it, two chairs, and a sofa. I felt more timid than before, and it seemed as though every muscle twitched as I followed his direction to sit in a nearby chair. After a brief period of questions, for which I offered one or two-word replies, there was no more dialogue. Silence hung in the air like an unexpected fart, and I grew more uncomfortable as I noticed him staring at me. I glanced at him and then dropped my gaze to the floor. If I had anything to share, he was going to have to pull it out of me. Much of the session was spent with him talking to me about medication, but I would have nothing to do with it. Simply being there was already so far outside my comfort zone; drugs were definitely out of the question.

Most of what I noticed was his penetrating eyes, which burned with intensity as though he was forcing himself to see inside my head. And his *voice*, chipmunk-like with his Guyanese accent.

Dr. Styena asked if he could play a recording for me. I shrugged as if to say, "I don't care one way or the other." He opened a drawer and pulled out his cassette player, and then out of another drawer he took a small cassette tape. He loaded the machine and hit the "play" button, then leaned back in his chair and watched me. For the next forty-five minutes, I listened to the crazed voice of Reverend Jim Jones preaching messages of absolution to nine hundred of his followers in the jungle of Guyana, instructing them to commit acts of "revolutionary suicide" while they stood in line to drink the sugary poisonous mixture from metal vats. I listened to his sometimes incoherent ranting. I listened to people shouting and screaming. I listened to children crying. I listened to gunfire in the distance (Jones's "soldiers" were instructed to shoot anyone who tried to escape through the jungle). After the cries vanished and the screaming eventually stopped, what I listened to next was the sound of a single gunshot, presumably Jones's own suicide. Then, for several minutes while the tape was still running, I listened to silence.

While the tape played, the little doctor watched me. I sat in the chair next to his desk and said nothing. When the tape was finished, he asked if I had any reaction. I did not. I was well aware of what happened in the jungle that November afternoon two years before because I had closely followed the news coverage, but in his office that day, I felt absolutely nothing.

At the end of the session, I agreed to come back. *What do I have to lose?* I thought. My strength was drained, my hopes were dwindling, and my options were, at best, rapidly fading.

By the end of the second session, I gave in and agreed to take the medication. By now, he was sitting next to me on the sofa, explaining how to take it. He asked if I had any questions. I had only one: "Can you overdose?"

He looked at me and said, "I can't believe you asked me that."

Our appointments were moved to his home office so I could see him in the evenings after work. His large, messy house didn't fit in amongst the more elaborate Victorian mansions with their manicured lawns that lined his street on Upper Mountain Avenue. On the first evening, I parked on the street and rang the doorbell. A small child of about six years old answered the door and directed me through the foyer and into a waiting area off to the right. The doctor's office was through the double doors beyond there. The kitchen was visible toward the back of the house, and I was uncomfortable peering into his personal living space.

After a few minutes, Dr. Styena opened the double doors and invited me in. Another patient walked past me on her way out, and I was embarrassed for both of us at the lack of privacy. The office had several chairs of varying size and design, a stereo system, and a sofa, upon which perched a small rectangular pillow with a needlepoint design that read "When Life Gives You Lemons, Make Lemonade." For an hour, I sat in a wooden chair facing him, my arms folded across my chest and my legs wrapped tightly together. He stared at me while my gaze shifted from him to the floor, to the walls, to the lemonade pillow, and back to him. I said very little. My voice was stuck. My breath was shallow. I didn't like being there. I didn't trust it. He kept staring, those piercing bug-eyes boring a hole through me. At the end of the hour, I left. Two nights later, I was back. Repeat of the first night. Same chair, same posture, same tightness in my chest. But this time, he started asking questions. About my job, my boyfriend, my sex life. "None of your business," I told him.

I didn't trust him, and I certainly didn't feel comfortable in his presence, and yet in a strange way, I still felt attached to him. I hoped he could help me, and that's why I kept returning. That, and mistaking the sick feeling I had in my gut as being a normal apprehension of psychotherapy. I pushed on. After all, I had no other options and, this time, nowhere to run.

Seven months of three-times-a-week sessions, and I was still living in darkness, exacerbated by the debilitating effects of all the medication he was prescribing. Pills to lift my mood, pills to reduce anxiety, pills to help me sleep. He told me I needed them, and I complied, too tired and weak to argue. The antidepressants were the worst. MAO inhibitors and tricyclics were the only available drugs on the market, and their side effects rendered me a zombie.

Most sessions consisted of the same scenario played over and over. I arrived. I sat, folding into myself. I kept quiet. He stared, asking an occasional question (the topic of which often involved sex). Then one night he suggested doing something different. He told me about something called sodium amytal, which is a type of truth serum. He explained that I would be able to answer questions but wouldn't remember any of it. I could deal with that, since I was more afraid of hearing myself tell him things than allowing him to know anything that may have been a secret even to me.

I was to meet him the following Tuesday morning in his office in Newark where I had gone for my first few appointments. He explained that this was a safe venue because oxygen was nearby should I have a reaction. Another woman, presumably a doctor, was in the room when I arrived. While I was too frightened to ask why she was there, it did give me a level of comfort knowing I wouldn't be alone with him. He instructed me to lie back on a reclining chair, and he inserted an IV into my right arm. He then held his finger in the air and told me to follow it with my eyes. It moved around in front of my field of vision, then up and over my head where he now stood behind me. I strained my eyes to see past my forehead, and then I remember nothing after that.

I woke up several hours later. Groggy and nearly paralyzed by fatigue, I looked around the room to get my bearings. It took me a moment to realize my shirt was disheveled. An explosion of fear, anger, and rage that had been stuffed inside me erupted in a violent outpour that I had never felt before. Along with that came an enormous wave of grief that engulfed me, and I curled up into a fetal position and cried and cried … and cried more. Dr. Styena sat next to me, his hand in mine. The woman who had been there earlier was gone. The tears kept coming.

I started babbling. And babbling. No filter between my brain and mouth. It all came out.

Out spilled anger, out spilled grief, out spilled my broken heart. Every nerve fiber was on fire, and my chest was heaving with every breath. I didn't realize how much I was holding inside. After some time passed, I quieted down, and he managed to help me out of the recliner and out the door as I watched the room spin around and around. Clearly, I was not driving myself home, so he put me in his car, and I managed to slur directions clear enough to lead him to my house forty-five minutes away.

That night, Walter sat in a chair across the room and watched me thrashing in my sleep.

By morning I wasn't well enough to go to work. Dr. Styena called, and I lay in bed as we talked for a long time. The conversation was light as we talked about everyday things. He told me how he got into psychiatry and said he didn't like being a surgeon because he felt like a mechanic. I laughed. It seemed okay to be talking with him like this, almost natural. For now, I forgot who he was to me. For now, he was my friend.

The next morning, I still didn't feel right. Rather, something felt very wrong. The effects of the sodium amytal had worn off but left in its wake a sense of being naked, exposed, and very afraid. I called my boss and said I wouldn't be coming to work, and that I don't know when I would be back. Out of sheer impulse, I drove to the airport and got on a plane to Miami. Maybe if I ran away (again), I could forget.

I called some friends when I arrived and they invited me to stay with them. That night, the phone rang. It was *him* again. He had learned where I was and wanted to find out what happened.

"Why did you leave?"

"I don't know."

"Where are you staying?"

"With friends."

"I want to come down there."

I was struck by this last statement. Who would do that? Maybe I should have been suspicious. Maybe I should have told him not to. Maybe I should have fired him. All the things I *should* have done, I didn't do. What I did instead was tell him I'd meet him at the airport. At the time, I thought that any doctor who would go this far out of his way for a patient was someone special. It would be years before I could clearly see how wrong it all was. My parents weren't around to protect me, and I certainly wasn't in my right mind, so who would stop him? I was so desperately lonely at the time that in my twisted perspective, I saw him not as a rogue but as a savior.

We left the airport in his rental car, and he drove to a nearby hotel that had a bar, where we spent the next several hours. One drink was followed by the next, he was ordering for both of us. I got drunk, and he cried over his childhood. Of course I felt sorry for him. Of course it was sad how his wealthy father gave him nothing as a boy. Of course this entire afternoon scenario seemed completely normal to me at the time.

Evening approached, and it so happened that his nephew lived nearby, so we drove to his house. He didn't seem fazed about my presence, which lends itself to the probability that I wasn't the first psychiatric patient—or young woman—his uncle had brought to his home. In my drunken, medicated naiveté, I simply went along with it all.

The four of us got comfortable in the living room. Dr. Styena, me, nephew, and nephew's wife. I was still feeling the effects of the afternoon binge drinking, and I sat curled up tightly in a chair while I watched the the nephew pull out a plastic bag from his drawer and place it and a small envelope of rolling papers on the coffee table. He took out one small rectangle of paper, sprinkled marijuana into it, rolled it tightly, licked the long end to seal it shut, and lit the end of it. He and Dr. Styena shared the joint while I sat frozen in my chair, inhaling the sweet odor wafting around the room.

It was late, and neither of us was in any capacity to drive. Mr. and Mrs. Nephew eventually went to bed, leaving Dr. Styena and me alone in the living room. He sat on the edge of a chair, shoulders slumped, gazing at the floor. "I didn't come here to fuck you," he said. The words stung like a taser. He kept saying it over and over, and each time, I recoiled more. I was repulsed. *Why is he saying this? I don't understand where this is coming from.* I needed to get away but had nowhere to go, so I pushed myself out of the chair, staggered down the hall, and found a spare room on the right. I locked the door and stayed there for the rest of the night.

"I want to bring you back and put you in the hospital," he told me the next day.

"I don't know if I'm coming back," I said.

Even though I still held on to the misguided sense of being taken care of, he was approaching a boundary that I didn't want him coming near. "Caring" for me was one thing, but knowing where his mind really was had pushed me to the verge of panic.

In the end, I struck a deal with him where I would stay in Miami for a few more days and then allow him to admit me to the hospital when I returned.

It was a small hospital on another side of Montclair, miles away from the teaching hospital in Newark, where his office was and where there was a large psychiatric unit. This gave him easy access to come and go—which he did often and at late hours—without raising the eyebrows of his colleagues. He admitted me to a regular patient unit and asked the nurses to put me in a private room. I wasn't sure why I was even there but neither did I ask; I assumed he knew what he was doing.

He brought me food and chocolate.

He stayed late into the night, chatting.

He was caring for me, right? Didn't he do this with all of his patients?

Or was I special? Because I sure felt that way.

One day about a week into my stay, he offered to sign a day pass so I could leave for a few hours. I loved Manhattan and wanted to spend the day there, and he invited himself along. Not only did I not object, but I was glad he would be my companion. I took him to my favorite Greek restaurant on Bleecker Street and to my favorite dance club in midtown. We were out well into the night and long past hospital curfew, but neither of us seemed to notice or care.

About 2 a.m. I was getting tired and asked him to take me back to the hospital. The route out of Manhattan from midtown took us through the Lincoln Tunnel into Weehawken. I wanted to show him my favorite view of the Manhattan skyline, which was particularly beautiful at night, so we took the first exit at the top of the ramp and turned right toward Hamilton Park along the Hudson River. He parked the car on the street and we walked through the park toward a fence at the top of a cliff that overlooked the river and the city beyond. We stood looking across, when he turned toward me, took my face in his hands, and leaned in to kiss me. I jumped back, startled and repelled.

"What the hell are you *doing?*" I shouted. "I don't want *that* from you!"

"I know you want me. In fact, I know you better than you know yourself," he squeaked.

"That's bullshit!" I shouted as I turned and ran toward the car, him following close behind. We drove back in silence, and when he pulled into the hospital parking lot, I quickly got out of the car and slammed the door behind me. I ran upstairs into my room and dove into bed fully clothed, pulling the covers over my head.

He came to my room the next day, and nothing was mentioned of what happened the night before. I had to admit that I *had* grown attached to him, but having any kind of close relationship was so far from any realm of possibilities that I couldn't bring myself to even address what he had done. I left the subject alone and hoped it would be forgotten by us both.

After two weeks, I left the hospital and moved in with friends while Walter found another place to live. I could barely tolerate his presence anymore and said I wouldn't go home until he was gone. My friends' house was close to where Dr. Styena lived, and I could easily get there for my three-times-a-week appointments. Large quantities of medication and extreme drowsiness notwithstanding, I managed to drive myself to my next appointment. As I sat in my usual chair not offering much in the way of dialogue, I found it was getting difficult to stay awake and asked to lie down for a few minutes. I don't remember falling asleep.

I was awakened by the feeling of movement. Confused and disoriented, I didn't initially register what was happening. But then I knew: he was pulling my clothes off. I struggled against him, but the drugs had a hold on me and I was weak.

"No! No!" I tried to scream, but only whispers came through. The words were trapped inside my throat.

"It will ruin everything! *No! Please!*"

He didn't stop.

I couldn't fight.

I tried to push back against his thrusts, and when he was done, he climbed off and sat on the sofa. I slowly stood up and struggled to pull my pants back up. I moved in slow motion, trying to wrap my mind around what had just happened. As I struggled to dress, I glanced at him. Once again he had that familiar posture of slouching, head slumped, gaze down.

I couldn't believe what had just happened. In an instant, everything changed. He had finally crossed a line that was chiseled in stone, and it couldn't be undone. Figuratively speaking, he was now naked.

I should have run.

I should have called the police.

I should have slugged him.

I should have done so many things, but the only thing I *did* do was feel sorry for him.

"It's okay," I whispered to him. In my medicated state of mind, I was feeling bad that he was feeling bad. *I* was consoling *him*.

The only journal entry I made later that night read:

April 18
RAPE
It's not real, is it?

Outside the realm of all sensibility, I continued to see him. I told myself that he loved me and that's why he did what he had done that night. I even told myself that he would divorce his wife, leave his four children, and marry me. It didn't matter that he wanted sex during our sessions or that he said, "You have to lie for me," when he learned that my uncle was asking questions about him at the college where he taught. Nor did it matter that he gave me Quaaludes, knowing I wouldn't object to sex if I was sedated, telling me, "They're just aspirin," because after all, he loved me. And I let myself believe him when, after a suicide attempt six months later, he came to the hospital and told me, "You just didn't do it right."

But some things he said were clearly ridiculous, and I told him as much.

"Bullshit!" I said when he claimed, "I *have* to have sex with you for you to get better." That comment tipped the scale of my suspended disbelief and I knew it was pure garbage, but I still stayed with him. In a sense, I was addicted to him and he knew it. Being parentless, depressed, and the sole caretaker of a younger brother who was as lost as I was created a perfect storm for him to parade over the clear and well-established boundaries set forth by the oath he had chosen to ignore.

I also learned a lot about his other patients, who he freely discussed by name.

"Rita Johannsen keeps gaining weight because she is afraid of men."

"Mr. Hockler drinks too much but is keeping it a secret from his family."

"Mrs. McCleary's son is a real pain in the ass."

"You know, I just can't stand some of my patients."

I felt embarrassed for these people, having an uninvited voyeuristic glance into the secrets they shared with him. But I never considered that he was also telling them about me. He wouldn't do that because, after all, he loved me.

He liked to play music during our sessions, which sometimes included sex (he billed me for those sessions anyway, and I paid for them anyway) and sometimes consisted of us sitting in his office, having cocktails (paid for those sessions, too). One of his favorite songs was from Pink Floyd's *The Wall* album. When the words sang, "Is there anybody out there?" he pointed to my head, laughing, and sang, "Is there anybody *in* there?"

He fixed his round, chocolate eyes on me, and I felt him studying me, turning me upside down, shaking me, and placing me back to see what was left. All with a smile on his face and a rum and coke in his hand.

Two months after my suicide attempt, I arrived for a session one afternoon particularly distraught. I sat across from him curled into a ball, head hung, arms and legs wrapped tightly, and cried. "I need help!" I pleaded. I knew he had to see my pain and know how much I was hurting. In that moment, I believed he would hit the pause button on our relationship and offer his most professional wisdom, guidance, and compassion that would for sure finally help me begin to heal.

He stood up, walked over and sat on my lap, and drove his tongue into my throat. I pushed him off with such force that the sound of him tumbling to the floor was heard in the waiting room.

I threw open the door and left, running past the wide-eyed stares of his next patient. When he called me two days later, I listened to him yell at me for embarrassing him in front of his patient.

Our relationship continued for more than a year, but it just didn't feel right. I wasn't getting better. In fact, I was getting worse. Much worse.

The unerring barometer of my mental decline was the increasing challenge of doing most anything, from getting out of bed in the morning, to functioning at work, to finding any amount of satisfaction in the simple act of eating a meal. The grayness of my world persisted. The weight of my depression was crushing me. My body carried the heaviness of a circus elephant, my limbs were moving in slow motion through space, my breath barely made it in and out of my body, and the wrenching ache in my heart was visceral. I wanted to find a mountain and crawl to the top and scream out my pain. I wanted to punch myself stupid just so I would feel *something*. But I kept silent because no one could help me.

Access to hope had been repudiated often enough, and I was finally giving up.

When you make the decision to end your life, you experience a peculiar sense of calm. Nothing can bother you because nothing matters. The decision can be thought out over time or made in the moment. My decision had been brewing for weeks, and when the day came, I knew it.

I'll show him.

My friends will have to get along without me.

Joey will have to get along without me.

I will be done.

I will be no more.

The pain of being alive was so intense that removing myself from existence became the only option I had left.

I drove to my evening appointment with Dr. Styena. On the way, I swallowed all the pills I had in my purse. Quaaludes, sleeping pills, antidepressants, even heart medication for whatever God-knows-why reason, whatever he had given me went into my stomach. My plan was to get to his house, tell him good-bye, and drive to a remote area and park my car. I'd be there long enough before anyone would find me, so I would have enough time to die.

The pills were already taking effect by the time I got to his house. It had become difficult to walk once I was inside, so I quickly sat down in my usual chair. The room began to move in a figure-eight pattern, and in the center was him sitting in his chair, staring at me. I kept telling him nothing was wrong, that I had to leave. But I couldn't because my body was glued to the chair from the double g-force gravity brought on by the drugs. He left the room then reappeared a few minutes later. By now I was floating in and out of consciousness. Some time had passed before I heard shouting in the foyer.

My friends Sam and Denis were there. He had called them to come get me. Denis ran in and knelt in front of me. He peeled open my eye, took a look, and ran back out. More shouting, then I fell unconscious.

I woke up in a bed one, maybe two days later, covered in white sheets with wires that snaked out from underneath that attached to machinery nearby. The room was still moving. Although my arms felt like lead, I managed to drag one of them across my belly. I pulled the wires off the probes that were stuck to my chest, which made the machine's alarm sound. Running footsteps that got louder stopped at the side of my bed. A nurse reattached the wires and then left. Again, my arms moved at glacial speed to pull the wires off. And again, Nurse Running Feet appeared and reattached them. I'm pretty sure she put my hands in restraints.

Days passed as I became more coherent. Denis came to the hospital and told me how close I had actually been to dying. "Your status was critical," he said. He said he had argued with Dr. Styena about him giving me Quaaludes (which he denied), about having sex with me (which he denied), about being the one responsible for my suicide attempt (which he denied).

Denis had driven me to the hospital and carried me into the emergency room; Dr. Styena just wanted me out of his house.

Once recovered and home again, I began to see with more clarity that Dr. Styena really wasn't interested in helping me after all. The only time he was attentive was when he wanted sex. One time he rented a hotel room and apparently had high expectations. I wasn't in a good place emotionally, and all I could really do was escape into sleep. I was lying in bed with the covers over my head, listening to him stand next to me and cry, "C'mon. I've been sick and haven't had any. Once I get it up, I can't get it down again!"

Without the energy to fight with him about it, I rolled onto my back and lay motionless while he climbed into bed and performed sex on me. Afterward, with no hesitation or evidence of concern, he proceeded to tell me why I couldn't orgasm, the reason which had nothing to do with him.

By then I knew he was hurting me. An inner teacher who I would not meet for years was telling me that this relationship was very, *very* wrong. It was telling me I needed to heal, I needed help. And I wasn't going to get it from him. Ever. It became all too clear to me that he never had any interest in helping me; his motives were completely self-serving. So I began to pull away. I stopped making appointments and stopped calling him. The last time we spoke was months later when he called. He was having heart trouble and had been in the hospital for several days and was looking for a sympathetic ear. If there had been any amount of compassion toward him before, it was now gone. In a matter-of-fact tone, I wished him well and said good-bye.

By then, I was relieved to be free of him.

I didn't realize at the time that I was bound within the confines of an illusion I had created, with his help, where I believed that there was nothing wrong with our relationship. Even his live-in housekeeper who made breakfast for us each morning when his wife and children were in Europe didn't so much as bat an eye as she poured my coffee and served me poached eggs. So why would I think anything was amiss?

Much later when I tried to make sense of the dynamics behind his behavior and mine, I learned of something called transference. In psychoanalytical terms, it's taking emotions we experience in childhood and shifting them onto another person, and is often seen when a patient transfers feelings she'd had for a parent or other adult figure onto a therapist. It's a very common phenomenon and one that is taught in mental health training. Psychiatrists and psychotherapists are very familiar with this concept and are trained to deal with patients who exhibit feelings of transference. They help the patient work through her (or his) feelings while maintaining healthy professional boundaries.

It was even covered years later during my training as a yoga therapist. But at the time, I wasn't aware of why I felt so drawn to him, even in the aftermath of the assault. He should have clearly understood that transference was playing out in the dynamics of our patient-therapist relationship, maybe because of whatever I had confessed while under the sodium amytal, and he should have honored the concrete boundaries in place between us. But I guess he wasn't paying attention in school the day they taught the Hippocratic Oath.

An Unexpected Joy

Surprise is the greatest gift which life can grant us.

—Boris Pasternak

I began to hear the call once again. A year after my relationship with Dr. Styena ended, I decided to once again try making a new life in California. Joey had enlisted in the army after high school, so that left me free to live anywhere. I was now twenty-four and saw my life ahead as an open road that would take me anywhere the wind blew, so I decided to enroll in a private art college in Santa Barbara to pursue my growing interest in photography.

I drove out of Denville on a July morning in a van I purchased that had all the necessary comforts built into it to make the journey cozy: a cushioned bed, paneled walls, and sconce lights that I used for reading at night. I was living off my savings, and my budget prevented the luxury of hotels, so the van and the kindness of friends who allowed me to park in their driveways would be my accommodations for most of the trip.

After three weeks on the road with stops in Ohio, Iowa, Wyoming, Reno, and San Francisco, I arrived in Santa Barbara late at night to the scent of eucalyptus lingering in the air. *This is now my home*, I thought. I found the apartment I had sublet from a friend of a friend and began unloading the van. The apartment was above a row of garages tucked behind a series of small

Craftsmen-style houses on De La Vina Street. I walked up the uneven wood plank stairs on the side of the building, found the key under a planter, and unlocked the faded gray door. Entering into darkness, I felt up and down the wall next to the door and found the only light switch in the room. A bare bulb dangling from a wire that hung from the center of the ceiling sprang to life as my eyes adjusted to my surroundings. The entire apartment was essentially one room, and the lone ceiling light didn't do much to brighten it. Along the wall to my left was an old sofa that had seen a lifetime of use, the imprint of many fannies sunk into the vinyl cushions. To my right was a Murphy bed that was unfolded from the wall. Behind the wall was a small kitchen with white metal cabinets and an old white refrigerator, the kind with rounded edges and a stainless steel handle you pulled to pry the door open. To the left of the kitchen was a small bathroom that was tiled in 1950s green. The apartment was perfect.

Rain fell hard for several days, and I stayed inside most of the time. It was August, and school wouldn't be starting for a few weeks, so there wasn't much to do except walk to downtown and the beach. The few windows in the apartment weren't large enough to push the darkness out, and the dreariness seemed to penetrate my bones. After a week, the sun returned, but the dreariness remained. I could feel the depression creeping back like a slow-moving fog rolling over the California hills.

Why am I feeling this way?

This is where I wanted to live, and I was finally here, so why was I not happy? Fatigue weighed me down more than the remnants of last week's weather, so I made a point of going outside often. I walked along the beach and ate lobster at Sterns Wharf, window-shopped on State Street, drank wine on my porch in the evening, and discovered a farmers' co-op that offered the freshest produce in the region. Still, I found myself spending more time in bed than anywhere else. Maybe my subconscious intention to "just disappear," as I told a friend I had visited somewhere mid-country, was happening after all. My depression had caused me to be extremely tired in the past, but this felt slightly different. There was another component to it that I couldn't identify.

The small box I had bought on a whim sat unopened in the bathroom. There was, after all, no reason to have the slightest suspicion. Multiple partners—a sore replacement for the devastating emptiness I was living with—had never resulted in children, so I decided I must be barren. No problem, I didn't want kids anyway. My life had begun anew in this beautiful place, and despite how I was feeling, my focus was on building a new life here and leaving the painful memories of New Jersey far behind, once and for all.

But the fatigue persisted, so I decided to settle any doubts by opening the small package and peeing on the stick. *Just get it over with so you can stop thinking about it*, I thought. To my astonishment, what appeared in the tiny window—and what should have taken two hours—revealed in just minutes the result I never imagined: *I'm pregnant.* Disbelief mixed with joy mixed with fear clouded my mind as I hurriedly scanned the phone book to find the nearest women's clinic.

When I arrived, a quick blood test revealed what the tiny blue circle on the pee stick claimed. Still feeling the initial shock, I sat nervously as a young woman-girl entered the tiny consultation room.

She had in her hand several pamphlets on abortion: where to have one, what to expect, what it cost, and proceeded to "counsel" me on what my decision should really be, given that I wasn't married and all. Seeing the horror on my face, she shoved the pamphlets into my hand as I stood to leave. I walked out of the building, dropping the papers into the trash as I left.

The timing probably couldn't have been better and couldn't have been worse. My unexpected pregnancy had pulled me out of my depression, but I had also just enrolled in college and had no job and no health insurance. The only money I had was what was left over from my trip and from the sale of my van once I got to Santa Barbara. The bicycle I brought with me became my mode of transportation.

I called Walter to give him the news, and he drove out from New Jersey the following week. We had rekindled our relationship shortly before I left, and I had to fight against his criticisms about me leaving, such as telling me what a stupid idea it was to move away. I could see beneath his objections that he was just sad to see me leave, and maybe a little scared that I'd wind up in another cult, so I didn't hold it against him but I didn't let him stop me either.

When he first arrived in Santa Barbara, we fought constantly over every little thing except the elephant that was in the room with us. Maybe neither one of us was prepared to face such a monumental task, so we fought about everything else as a way to avoid the topic and having to make a decision about it. Enough time went by that the decision was made for us; I was too far along to do anything but carry the baby to term. Truth be told, that was the only decision I would have ever made.

Classes started in September, and I got a job cleaning houses. Walter spent most of his days at the beach while I went to class and worked on assignments in the photo lab at school. By early spring, we needed to decide what our next move would be. I was still feeling happy, no sign of the depression, so I felt safe making the decision to have the baby back in New Jersey, mainly because he had family there. Aside from a few casual friends I had made at school, I had no real support system in place in Santa Barbara, and the closest hospital that wasn't a detox or rehab center was far away. Walter had bought an old car with rusted floorboards to make the drive west, so after I handed in my assignments and took a leave of absence from school, we strapped most of my belongings onto the top and the back of our little car and headed east.

When we moved back to New Jersey, our intention was to have the baby and return to Santa Barbara within five months. What we couldn't fit into my car was left in storage under my apartment. The drive east was full of excitement as we stayed with friends along the way. It still hadn't sunk in that I was actually going to have a child; I was happy just to be pregnant.

I was in my eighth month when we arrived back in Denville late one March night. We moved into the tiny converted boathouse on Cedar Lake that Walter had rented before I left the previous summer. The total size of the place, including bedroom, bathroom, living area, and kitchen, was no more than one hundred eighty square feet, but it offered a serene view from a large window onto the lake. My prenatal care in Santa Barbara was through the local clinic that didn't cost anything. Once in New Jersey, I found a midwife who agreed to deliver the baby for a significantly reduced fee.

The night I went into labor, I was almost three hours from home. I had driven to Philadelphia to see Walter, who was there on a temporary job. The woman who put him up while he was in town invited me to stay the night because I wasn't feeling well. I tried sleeping, but the feeling of indigestion kept me awake. Around 11:30, I sat up in bed, holding my belly. Our hostess came into my room, saw the look on my face, and said, "Do you have pain down your legs?"

"Yeah," I grunted, bending over the bed.

"Honey, you're in labor."

Oh my God, I thought. *This is really happening.* I was scared and afraid of what was ahead. I was too young and immature to be a mother, and I knew absolutely nothing about taking care of babies.

Besides, the patience needed to raise a child was a virtue I didn't possess in any amount. Throughout my pregnancy, my joy was over the fact that I really could get pregnant, and I failed to see the reality of what lay beyond that. But there was no turning back now.

Walter threw his things in the car while I paced, or rather, limped around the living room. We left the house around 12:30 a.m. He drove with one hand on the steering wheel and timed my contractions, holding a stopwatch in his other hand. I tried sleeping for a few hours at home and then phoned Jean, my midwife, who told us to meet her at the hospital. I didn't want to go because going would mean I'd really have the baby. In my skewed thinking, if I could stay home, the pain would stop and life would go on as normal.

At the hospital, as the contractions grew more intense, I grew more frightened. Hours into my labor, I asked for an epidural, but Jean said it was too late. All the breathing my Lamaze classes taught me went out the window, and I found myself fighting against a strong current of forward momentum. Instead of going with it, I resisted. After several hours, a doctor appeared in the doorway.

"Things are not progressing. We may have to do an emergency C-section on you," Jean said. I knew I had to stop fighting and allow nature to takes its course; I wasn't going to win this battle. With everything I had in me, I let my body soften and felt torrential waves of pain wash through me, over and over, as I gasped for breath like a beached mammal drowning in the rising surf.

At 8:40 that evening, and after twenty-five hours of labor, I took one last deep breath, bore down as hard as I could, and screamed until my daughter's little body squeezed out of me.

Within days, the fear of motherhood and the responsibility of taking care of a newborn subsided, and I settled in to caring for her. We named her Leala, and the sun rose and fell each day on her. I lay in my bed with her tiny body swaddled in softness and got busy loving her.

It's Dark at the Bottom

No man ever steps in the same river twice, for it's not the same river and he's not the same man.

—Heraclitus

We never did return to Santa Barbara. Walter was getting sporadic work, and I had formed a close bond with new friends, so we let life take over and didn't talk about moving. Besides, I felt that by then, New Jersey had more to offer me than California did, and I wasn't about to leave the life I was growing to trust. A year later, we moved out of the boathouse into a two-bedroom converted bungalow in the woods on the other side of the lake. I was happy to finally have space to move around and got busy hanging wallpaper, painting Leala's bedroom, and making our little place a home.

But by the time my daughter was two years old, the depression had fully resurfaced. I didn't ever expect it to return, but the slightest variation in my sense of well-being sent strong warning signals that it was creeping back into my soul. This time it came with a vengeance. It sucked the very life out of me, rendering me weaker, more distanced from what gave me joy, until I became a hollow shell of my former self.

The internal dialogue that was going on inside my head fueled my despair, which only served to affirm that what I was telling myself was true. The suffering that was my punishment was just. I had failed as a daughter, I failed as a sister, and I failed as a partner. It became a vicious cycle of telling myself this, which made the depression worse, which confirmed the story I was telling myself. To add to it, I was wrestling with memories of Dr. Styena, which created anger so intense that at times I was blinded by it. I waffled between despair and rage, taking it out in bouts of fury onto the pages of my journal.

"HELP ME HELP ME HELP ME ... I'M SLOWLY DYING DYING DYING DYING"

These words appeared before me as my pen bit into the paper.

> *"I'm on the verge of exploding. I don't know how to let it out. God, this is a nightmare! These words I write can never express what I truly feel. I hate I love I hate I love I hate I love hate love hate love hate YOU!! You know who you are, you fucker! You know what you really are! THIS IS NOT THE END OF IT. YOU'LL SEE. I'LL SEE YOU AND YOU'LL KNOW WHAT YOU ARE AND WHAT YOU DID AND HOW YOU SO CRUELLY BETRAYED ME AND HOW I LOVED YOU SO AND HOW I STILL LOVE YOU SO AND HATE YOU SO.*
>
> *I won't commit suicide, but there is a silent suicide. No will to live. The heart dies and the body eventually follows. It's not so visible that way. It's already begun. Happiness was meant for other people, not me. Is the intensity clear? Somebody help me."*

I knew no one could ever help me because I allowed no one to read this.

For the next four years, an assortment of therapists and just as much medication—some good, some not so good on both accounts—failed to give me back my life. A variety of diagnoses and their accompanying pharmaceuticals included bipolar disorder, borderline personality disorder, schizophrenia, temporal lobe epilepsy, and major depressive disorder. My identity was reduced to a series of numbers, codes out of the *Diagnostic and Statistical Manual of Mental Disorders.* I was no longer Suzanne Ludlum; I was 296.34 and 301.83.

I was also hospitalized several times during this period. As my depression and despair grew stronger, the things that had once given me joy faded away like a face withdrawing into fog. I stopped eating. I stopped smiling. I stopped caring. I slept a lot. I lay in bed and willed myself to die. I offered no reaction when Walter stood over the bed, yelling at me, "You're sick! You're fucked up!"

All throughout this period, I tried with everything I had to be a good mother, but it became more difficult to even fill that role. In the beginning, I was fully engaged in Leala's life. I took her on outings and to playgroups. I prepared her meals. I fixed her hair and bought her pretty clothes. I walked her to the bus stop each morning and was there in the afternoons when she came home. I climbed into her bed each night to sing songs to her and to read her stories until we both fell asleep.

She was the one spark left that could ignite the joy in my soul, but I could feel even that extinguishing. I was falling again and didn't have a safety net to catch me. I found it impossible to do even the simplest of things and spent most of my days in bed. Now Leala climbed into my bed for stories and songs because I didn't have enough energy to move. Sometimes she just stood next to my bed and held my hand.

"Mommy, can you please sing to me?" she quietly asked.

With effort, I drew the air in and let my breath carry the words out of my mouth in a whisper:

"You are my sunshine, my only sunshine
You make me happy when skies are gray.
You'll never know dear, how much I love you,
Please don't take my sunshine away."

"I love you, Mommy."

"I love you, too, honey," my words squeaked out, barely audible. Leala said good-night and left the room as I lay there watching her go, hating myself for what I had become, yet feeling paralyzed by my inability to do anything about it.

I had now failed as a mother, too.

I told myself I didn't have any right to live, that the best years of my life were already behind me. I was A Sick Person, and nothing could save me. I would have mourned the death of my soul, but I simply didn't care enough.

The person who had once been me was buried so deep inside by then that I couldn't remember her or who she had been. I only knew she was gone. I was falling into a chasm that would take hold of what was left of the person who used to be me and hurl her into a dimension unreachable by anyone.

This is what a psychotic break feels like.

I woke up one morning feeling even more disconnected than usual. I hated waking up because it was like going back into the nightmare. Sleep became my coping strategy. If I wasn't awake, I wasn't aware. But the double-edged sword was that when I closed my eyes, a freight train appeared, barreling toward me. Behind my closed eyes, I once again became Alex DeLarge, only this time both witnessing and experiencing the violence so graphically displayed on the screen in front of him. I was a hostage in and of my own mind. And when my eyelids sprang open, I saw that I was waking up to the real nightmare that was my life.

That morning when my eyes opened, I remembered again that I was still alive, but I felt the last remaining ounce of will slipping away. An invisible weight descended upon my body and held it down. My body would not move as though I was glued to the bed. It was a feeling beyond heaviness. I knew my right arm extended out to the side and my left elbow bent with the back of my hand resting on the pillow. My left leg was there but also not moving, while my right foot dropped off the side of the bed and hung in space. My breathing was shallow and labored and barely perceptible to an onlooker. The sounds of the house waking up— Leala playing, dishes being washed in the kitchen sink—floated in through the bedroom door as I lay frozen, but they were muffled by an invisible vapor that lingered between them and me as though I was hearing the world from inside another dimension. I have no recollection of how long I lay motionless in that position. My brain had shut down.

Most of that day passed, and I eventually managed to contract my muscles enough to get my body moving. I crawled over to a Bentwood rocker next to the window, where I sat curled up, my eyes transfixed on a point on the ceiling over my head, hypnotized by the sound of the rocker moving back and forth, back and forth, against the hardwood floor. A moment later I felt the sensation of being sucked backward into a vortex of spacelessness. I waffled between feeling my body sitting in the rocker and not feeling my body at all. Was I even breathing?

I sensed a presence in the room but couldn't make out who was there. They weren't exactly human—spirits, maybe? *I can't let them see me*, I thought. They were watching me, always watching me. I was frozen in fear. I was safe in my room, my neutral ground. I sat, staring at the ceiling, completely immobile except for my right foot that rested on the floor, pushing and pulling my weight to create the rhythmic motion of rocking. I couldn't close my eyes; they were frozen open. Saline liquid began to stream out of them, down my cheeks, dropping onto my shirt, the room taking on the focus of a van Gogh painting. I was sinking into a dimension of no-time, further away from an existence I could no longer identify as my life.

Occasionally, my peripheral vision would pick up on my surroundings—the furniture, the earth-tone striped wallpaper that I'd hung when we first moved in, the soft light glistening through the window to my right, and Walter—who occasionally walked in—look intently at me, wave his hand in front of my face, and, seeing no reaction to his presence, let out a sigh, turn around, and leave the room. All the while, my eyes were still transfixed on that point on the ceiling as the saline dripped out of them. I hadn't blinked in more than an hour. A face! *Did I see that? Who are you? What are you doing up there?* As I struggled to look away, it remained there, periodically fading and then reappearing with a monstrous expression staring back at me.

I was in a mental straightjacket, paralyzed by something far beyond my ability to control. Those beings, those creatures, were now outside my door, waiting for me. I couldn't see them but I *felt* them. In my mind's eye, I saw Gollum, the spindly, emaciated creature from *The Lord of the Rings*.

Something told me I had to move from where I was. My eyes still transfixed on the ceiling, I slowly felt my way toward the bed and, when close enough, collapsed onto it. I lay motionless, getting myself reoriented. The room was dead still. I now heard the faint sounds of children outside, and somewhere in the background, the phone was ringing. The room gradually began to move, turning around and around, picking up speed, as the walls undulated in and out, in and out. Then the bed lifted off the floor. I grabbed onto the sides just before it took off, with me clutching it, soaring through the air like a magic carpet ride to hell. I was screaming, but no one heard me. I then realized the screams were coming from inside my head. Still, the noise was deafening. It bounced off the walls of my brain, echoing like the shrills of a hawk deep in a canyon. My eyes rolled around in my head as I tried to maintain my equilibrium and pull my body out of its contorted, twisted shape. Then, in what seemed like a second, the bed came crashing to the floor again like Dorothy's house landing in Oz. Everything was still, and I felt myself lying flat, arms and legs spread out on the bed. I felt something pushing hard against me. *What's happening to me?* I silently cried. *I'm losing touch. Come back! Come back!*

I tried to get up—at first, I couldn't seem to make the connection from my brain to my muscles. Yet somehow, I began to move in what seemed like slow motion. I got as far as the edge of the bed, but my mind went to the creatures just outside my bedroom, waiting for me to make a move beyond the door, and terror gripped me once again. I could hear them laughing at me, snickering among themselves. I felt their presence so strongly, it was hard to believe that no one else could. I banged my head against the wall to knock the thought of them out of my mind, but this brought only momentary relief. I had to pee, but leaving my room was out of the question. So I managed to straddle the trash can next to the bed, pull down my jeans, squat, and relieve myself into the can.

I heard noises around me, but I could no longer discern what was real from what was imagined. I fell onto the bed again, lying motionless, waiting to die, as the last notion of where I was slipped away. After day had turned into night, Walter reappeared. He stood over the bed, looking down at the catatonic form that was me, and called my name. I was aware of his presence, yet unable to respond. He mentioned something about the phone and Dr.

Schultze, the psychiatrist I had been seeing for two years. He said the doctor wanted to talk to me and it was very important that I take the call. He put the phone to my ear as my breath carried the words "I'm sorry" out of my weakened body.

"So am I," replied the voice through the wire, "more than you'll ever know."

Walter left the room as quickly as he entered, with phone in hand. I heard his voice uttering into the phone, and I was now frightened. *Get out! Get out!* The voice inside my head screamed. The fear I suddenly felt sent adrenaline surging through my body, jolting me back into a state of semi-coherence. My eyes darted around the room, desperately looking for a place to hide. My movements were slow and mechanical as I made my way toward the center of the room. *I must move quickly,* I thought, because someone is coming for me. Without putting my shoes on, I headed for the window.

Quietly, I raised the window and then the screen. I extended my right leg through the opening, nudging my body between the window over me and the ledge below me, and hastily pulled my other leg through. I couldn't see how far I fell in the darkness and crash-landed on a metal ladder. Hearing this, Walter dropped the phone and ran toward the bedroom. I heard the panic in his voice as he desperately called out my name. There was no time for thought; I turned and ran from the house, heading for the woods and the darkness where I could hide.

Hours later, I was in psych emergency at the hospital. I hadn't gone far in the woods; Walter found me sitting on a rock and drove me to the emergency room. I was unresponsive and catatonic and barely able to answer questions with any measure of sensibility.

"Where are you right now?" the attendant asked.

"Venice," I replied. *What did I just say?*

I sat slumped in the chair, staring unblinkingly at the ceiling as water continued to stream out of my eyes.

The dialogue would have seemed normal if it weren't for the questions and answers being totally out of sync with each other, like two different conversations going on in opposite directions.

I was aware of the words coming from me but had no control over what I said. Like a puppet on a string, my actions were not my own. I was frightened and wanted to run but at the same time, I desperately hoped someone would save me.

I was admitted to 4B Unit (they don't call them "wards" anymore; it sounds too, well, mental). For the first two weeks, I stayed in my room on the fourth floor without speaking. I didn't cry; I didn't utter a sound. I pulled the mattress off the wooden bed frame and stood it on its side in the corner of the room, creating a fort of sorts, where I slept on the floor wrapped in hospital blankets. The soundless screams continued to echo inside my head until the only way to silence them was to throw my head against the radiator with the force of a wrecking ball. This provided a strange sense of relief, and the physical pain was a welcome release. The clanging noise of skull against metal flew through the halls like an alarm bell, and I could hear shoes slamming against the tiled floor as several nurses ran toward my room. A tall blond woman—I guess she was head nurse—dropped to her knees and locked my head between her hands as her eyes pierced mine.

"Sue! Sue! Stop!" she cried. I could see her eyes meeting mine, but my gaze drifted somewhere through her as though I was looking at a ghost. I slowly slipped out of her hold and crawled back to my corner on the floor behind the mattress wall.

This went on for three more days until I grew so tired that I lay in my corner without coming out. I had stopped eating before the hospital. I loathed myself and decided that starvation was a suitable punishment for being alive. I stayed in my room, lying in my corner. After another week, my blood pressure had dropped to a dangerous level, and conversation among the medical staff circled around the topic of intravenous feeding.

Around the third week, something began to shift. As I lay on my bed (I eventually put the mattress back on the frame), I heard my own voice inside my head speaking to Joey years ago.

If anything happens to Dad, you and I will stick together.

I remembered the day I said that to him. I remembered reaching across the table to take his hand and seeing the anguish on his young face. How could I leave him now? And how could I leave my little girl? I knew the agony of losing my mother too young, and I felt horrible thinking that I could easily do the same to my own daughter.

There are two people in this world who desperately need me, I thought. I have to be here for them.

I sat up and looked at my friend, who had come to see me.

Wearily, I managed to pull the words out of my throat, "I can't go on like this anymore."

The shift I'm talking about was the realization that I had just hit bottom. I was thirty-one years old and had spent ten years falling hard into an abyss that I believed with all my being was unrecoverable. I couldn't see a way out, but I also knew I couldn't stay where I was. The faces of my daughter and kid brother crystallized in front of me as though to say: *It's time to climb up.*

So I began the long journey with my first step: I pulled myself off the bed, walked down the hall to the community room, and ate my first meal in three weeks.

At the end of week four, I went home. The night I was taken to the hospital, Dr. Schultze had made what must have been a difficult decision to discontinue working with me. Before that, he had always told me that the hospital was a dangerous place. But to me, the danger was at home. That's because I no longer felt safe living with Walter. I didn't trust him. He made sure I took my medication, made sure Leala was fed, made sure the bills got paid—when I was sick. He did all these things during each period when I was deep in depression and couldn't take care of myself or anyone else. As my illness began to take hold again—which it did for extended periods of time each year—he gladly took over the running of our household and the managing of me.

But during my healthy periods, he was a different person. He became moody, critical, and very angry. Once during an argument when I mentioned his stack of unpaid parking tickets, he pushed me onto a chair and grabbed the collar of my shirt, his eyes wide with fury and his anger showing itself in the protruding veins in his neck and white-hot fist that he pulled back like an archer drawing back his bow.

"Stop it! Stop it!" he shouted. "I can't take it anymore!"

I just stared at him. I hadn't meant to upset him, but the hero's cape had fallen from his shoulders, and his humanness was exposed. In that moment I wondered if he felt better about himself when I was sick and vulnerable.

In the months after the last hospitalization, I began my slow journey of healing. I resumed classes at a local community college and threw my energy into my photography, oftentimes using the medium to express the sorrow I was finally allowing myself to get in touch with.

Self-portrait 1991

I also started looking beneath the surface of my own illness and began to consider that, perhaps in part, my repeated hospital stays were a way of getting away from Walter. As scary a place the psychiatric unit was, its locked doors provided a barricade I didn't have at home. Things were done his way or no way at all. I had considered exploring religion, hoping to find some small amount of strength and direction from teachings in the Bible. This was not allowed. Walter was a self-proclaimed born-again atheist, and talk of God and Jesus were subjects that were off-limits.

Sex was also horrific. Walter's attitude was that I was his whenever he wanted me, and if I turned down his advances, he found other ways to get gratification. Sex repulsed me, and Dr.

Schultze had told him countless times that I couldn't handle any sexual activity because of what Dr. Styena did to me, and expressed to him that it was critical to my healing that he leave me alone.

So instead, he waited until I fell asleep and then made his move. Sometimes I woke up in the middle of it and pushed him away. Sometimes, depending on my medication dosing, I didn't wake up at all, but I felt different *down there* the next morning.

And sometimes, I gave in to his advances because it meant he'd be tolerable to live with the next day. But after it was over, I would lock myself in our tiny bathroom and cry into the darkness, my body heaving to expel the memory and smell of him, while he slept in the next room, laid out on the bed unconscious like a satiated cat after devouring its kill.

This climb wasn't going to be easy.

I had come across an article that described what he did as marital rape. When I brought it to his attention, he merely looked at me and said, "Those are the breaks, honey." I knew then that he was dangerous and that he wasn't interested in helping me get well. He wasn't the source of my illness, but he certainly had fed into it to satisfy his own desires and insecurities.

I had to consider that the release of my feelings of anger, rage, and sadness was incompatible with my living situation with Walter. Or perhaps living with him and feeling the repression, helplessness, and anger perpetuated the same feelings I had in my childhood, compounded by the memories of Dr. Styena. Either way, I had to get away from him, I had to run. But with a small child and very little money, I didn't see a way out. Until the morning after he assaulted me again, when I fled the house with Leala holding my hand.

I left her with friends while I drove to Naomi, my new therapist's office, and was a wreck when I got there. I cried as I told her what had happened and she said, "You can't go back there. Is there anywhere you can stay tonight?"

I called a friend, and she invited me to stay with her and her family until I could find a permanent place to live. After camping out in their living room for several weeks, Leala and I eventually moved into a spare bedroom.

As the weeks passed, I began to feel safer and more whole. My new hosts were spiritual people and openly talked of God. At first it felt strange, but at the same time, I found it refreshing, and so I began attending church services with them. I wasn't completely comfortable with the idea of God yet but was relieved to finally have the freedom to explore an aspect of life that had been prohibited during my life with Walter.

I felt like a captive who had just escaped her captor, and the world began taking on brighter hues. But the improvement in my mental state was matched only by the intensity with which Walter tried to convince people of how sick I really was. He called several of our friends—including my boss—with the dire words "she's *very* ill. Just wait, she'll be back in the hospital within a month."

But I never did go back. The last time—when I hit bottom the previous year—had been the last time. I began to see that getting away from Walter was indeed what I needed to do. Like separating from my family years before, by getting away from him, I was saving my own life.

A Hole in the World

*It's so much darker when a light goes out than it
would have been if it had never shone.*

—John Steinbeck

When crisis hits, we turn to what helps us feel safe. For me,
that was my brother Joey. He was my father's son through and
through, and nothing seemed to rattle him. His calm demeanor
was matched by his willingness to accept people without judgment.
His coolness under pressure helped him survive the hardship of
Special Forces training.

Joey had been deployed during Desert Storm and returned
from the Persian Gulf in June, two weeks after I left Walter. He
was twenty-seven and I was thirty-two, and we became closer
than we ever had been. Our weekly phone calls were light and
relaxed, very different from years earlier when he would call me
in his drunken state of despair, sometimes leaving unintelligible
messages on my answering machine in the middle of the night.
Struggling with my own darkness, I couldn't be the big sister he
needed. Truth be told, he scared me. Partly because I couldn't
help, and partly because I could more clearly see his demons as a
reflection of my own.

But he seemed different now. And I felt more comfortable
about him as well. We talked about getting together later in the

summer. Aunt Lou had invited us to visit, and we were sharing stories about how much fun we were going to have with her at her lake house in South Carolina.

Two months after I left Walter, he stole Leala. We had remained amicable at first, sharing custody on a weekly basis. She lived with me for a few days then I brought her to stay with him, giving all of us shared time. One day he never brought her back. He erased all of the messages I left on the answering machine and didn't answer the phone when I called. I knew he was keeping her at the house where we had lived, but he changed the locks on the doors, locked the windows, and guarded the door. My panic grew as my contact with her rapidly disappeared. Fearing he would leave with her and I'd never see her again, I called the local women's shelter for help. I drove by the house day and night, hoping to see her. I managed to walk in once when the door was unguarded, but Leala stood in horror as she watched him drag me through the house and toss me into the shrubs by the front door. I frantically called Joey and begged him to help.

"I can have him taken care of," Joey said in his deep voice. He seemed a million miles away that day. "I have people in the area, and nobody will see anything."

Joey's Special Forces security clearance enabled him to get away with things ordinary people might not, and I knew what he meant. My stomach turned over as his words took shape in my mind. I had always known Joey to be a quiet soul whose only act of violence was shooting clay pigeons with my dad on the weekends. This was out of character, and I wondered if something in his Persian Gulf experience had changed him. I knew that I would be the target of suspicion if anything happened to Leala's father and, moreover, felt that she needed her father more than I wanted him to disappear.

"No, leave him alone," I replied.

Instead, I called an attorney and paid him the last of the money I had in my bank account to help me get her back.

I hadn't seen Joey since the year before he left for the Gulf, when we'd met up at a family reunion in the mountains of Kentucky. Those reunions were always difficult for me; being with extended family was a painful reminder of my own family members who were no longer there. An extra hotel room usually served as the central meeting place where family members caught up with each other's lives, added new names to the written family records book, and planned daily excursions. While I, on the other hand, spent the time crying in my hotel bathroom. I wasn't close to many people and felt more like an outsider than a family member. I guessed Joey felt the same way because he made an appearance, stayed for two days, and quietly left one morning without saying good-bye to anyone. I only knew he was gone by the note he left on my windshield. "Sue, it was great seeing you and everybody. Talk to you soon. Love, Joe."

I envied his ability to slip away undetected.

Joe said he wanted to come to New Jersey for a visit that autumn. His previous visits were rare and clouded with a mixture of sadness and unease. I knew he was struggling, but I couldn't help him. Because he didn't care for Walter, and we were still living together, he never stayed long. But this visit would be different. I was free at last, and we were both in a better place in our lives. For the first time since he was orphaned at fifteen, I wasn't worried about him. I listened closely as his words carried through the phone line from his apartment near Ft. Hood in Texas. The desperation his voice had so often betrayed seemed to be replaced by a sense of peace and self-assuredness. We laughed a lot and planned our visit with Aunt Lou. It was the closest thing to having a normal relationship with my brother that I'd ever had.

One Friday evening, I was home alone while Leala was visiting her father (we had arranged a visitation schedule through the attorney). The phone rang, and I picked it up. Joey's voice was on the other end.

"Hi, Sue."

"Hi, Joe," I replied. He didn't sound like his renewed self. "What's wrong?" I asked.

"I'm thinking of requesting an early out." That meant putting in a request to leave the army before his enlistment period was up. The military gave him purpose and focus, and I worried what he'd do without structure to guide him. I suggested he come to New Jersey the following week to think about it. We spoke a few minutes more, and he agreed to look into flights.

"I'll call you early next week, okay?" I said.

"Sure," he replied. I sensed an edge to his voice but didn't want to push. In the past when I'd talk to him about getting help, he'd always replied with, "Whatever problems I have, I can fix them myself." I left it alone.

The silence was broken when I asked, "Are you okay?"

"Yeah, I'm fine."

"I love you, Joe."

"Love you too."

I went to bed and put the conversation behind me.

The next day was Saturday and I awoke that morning with a new sense of aliveness. It was a crisp October morning. The sun was shining, and the air felt clean. I took Leala into Manhattan with my friend and her children and spent the day hopping between museums and cafes. That night, I had a date with my friend Edward. It was more like a "friend" date than a real date, since we had known each other for years. We hadn't seen each other for a while when we ran into each other in the Hoboken PATH terminal and agreed to meet up again soon. Over dinner we talked about our families; his brother and sister and his parents who still lived in Ohio. He then asked me about mine. I had never offered that my parents and sister were gone because I was always uncomfortable with the discomfort felt by those who asked. This time was no different, but I was more at ease with Edward, so I decided to let him in a little and briefly cover the main facts. "It's not so bad," I offered in an attempt to mitigate his discomfort. "I have my brother."

After dinner, Edward and I walked to his car that was parked high atop an overlook that offered a panoramic view of Manhattan. There had always been an element of attraction between us that we chose not to acknowledge, but this night, the heat of our sexual energy burned away the reigns that had previously tethered our mutual attraction. We hadn't quite made it to his car before we fell into an unbridled round of passion. We fell against the passenger door, legs wrapping around legs, and hands and lips feverishly groping. We managed to open the door and spill into the front seat. I couldn't get enough of his full, wet lips and heated body against my jeans, and we continued in our tangled mess until exhaustion forced us to peel away from each other and find our breath. We hadn't gone much further than kissing, but that night with my friend was more charged than most full sexual encounters I'd had in the past. He eventually drove me to my car, and I wobbled over to it with a giggle and a smile. I felt dizzy with passion. I was definitely going to see him again.

I arrived at work the following Tuesday still recovering from my date.

"I feel so *alive!*" I declared to my friend Barbara. It must be the freedom I felt since escaping Walter. Maybe it was the surprised reawakening of my libido. Maybe it was a general sense that my life was starting anew and Grace was offering me another chance.

The phone rang. It was my friend with whom I was staying and she said two men wearing army uniforms had come to the house looking for me.

"*What?* He must have gone AWOL," I said with tightness in my throat. My fear was that Joey had packed his things and left on his own. *Why didn't he just put in his papers?*

"I need to call him."

I dialed a number that fed into Joey's unit at Ft. Hood, and an unfamiliar voice answered the phone.

"I'd like to speak with Sergeant Ludlum," I said.

"That's impossible," the male voice replied.

"Why?"

His words seemed to come through the wire in a matter-of-fact tone.

"He's deceased. Who is this?"

My breath seized, and then I screamed, "I'M HIS *SISTER!*"

A thunderbolt of shock surged through my body. I threw the phone down as my body fell back against the wall. My eyes lost their focus, and my lungs froze. Barbara ran into the room to see me sliding against the wall, my arms flailing to grab onto anything that would catch me, wide-eyed, speechless, and gasping for breath.

I heard someone crying, "No! No! No!" and then realized it was my own voice.

Together with another woman who heard the commotion, Barbara managed to get me to a chair in the corner of the office and sit me down. My entire body went lifeless. I slumped into the chair, my legs extended out on the floor and turned in different directions, my arms limp, and my head falling against the wall behind me. The two women held each of my hands as my cries faded into whispers and then into silence.

I must have left my body. I couldn't feel myself breathing or the chair under me. I have no recollection of time passing, but it must have been a while because the men who were at my friend's house eventually appeared in front of me.

One was an older man wearing a small gold cross on his lapel; the other was a stocky younger man with an expressionless face.

His eyes focused on the paper he held in his hands as I heard him read the words:

"The Secretary of the Army regrets to inform you that your brother is dead."

I felt the very life melt out of me at that moment, and I could hear the faint words off in the distance whispering again, *"no, no, no."*

I don't remember much about the ride home except that I was lying down in Barbara's car, clutching a photograph of Joey. He was leaning against a jeep in the Iraqi desert, his cap on backward, casually looking at the camera as if to say, "Yeah? So what. We're here. No big deal."

Later that day at home, I lay on the living room sofa. Barbara, Edward, and others I didn't know gathered around me. I lay in a catatonic state for several hours until a doctor friend of Barbara's arrived. He sat very close and leaned into my face. He talked about medication and hospitals, and I could feel his breath on my forehead. The more he talked, the more I felt anger rising in me until I leapt off the sofa, stomped into the bedroom, and kicked whatever my foot would aim for. I guess he figured his job was done, so he left.

Three days later, I boarded a plane to Killeen, Texas.

Joey's unit, the 47th EOD, planned a memorial service for him at Ft. Hood. I walked into the little chapel with Uncle Warren, Edward, and my friend Nancy, both of whom insisted on accompanying me to Texas, and found a seat among the sea of young men and women in uniforms, fidgeting in their chairs, not wanting to look at the face of the woman who reminded them of their comrade. Displayed in the front of the room were a pair of military boots, a rifle standing on end, and a helmet perched on top; I wondered if these belonged to Joey. I glanced at the folded service program that was handed to me and began reading about a young man I knew but really didn't know.

"He earned a *Bronze Star*?" I asked my friend sitting next to me.

He didn't even share the good things that happened in his life. A new layer of sorrow washed over me, thinking that if I had known about this honor when he was alive, I could have celebrated it with him, validated him, and had more time to show him how much I loved him. I guess he didn't care enough at that point to mention it. After the service, we were ushered into a back room, where several of Joey's friends lined up to speak with me.

"He's the last person any of us thought would ever do this," they said incredulously.

"Anybody but Joe."

"I can't believe it."

But I could. I knew how he could do it because his demons were my demons. We both were haunted by the same despair, the same depression, the same desperate loneliness. Only I suppose he felt that, in the end, he didn't have quite enough reason to stick around. Thinking back about that last phone call between us, the edge I sensed in his voice must have been him disengaging.

Later that evening, Joey's commanding officer, the casualty officer, and a few of his buddies from his unit went out for dinner and invited Edward, Nancy, Uncle Warren, and me to go. It was Halloween, and our restaurant was attached to a shopping mall where crowds of children were running and squealing as they collected baskets full of treats. I watched the people at my table distracted in conversation and noticed the group at the table next to us singing in celebration of a birthday. I was locked inside a bubble of isolation that was devoid of air and life, watching the world from inside this dead space and feeling immensely alone. The paradox of the nearby celebration mixed with the devastating emotions I was feeling was too much for me to bear, and I bolted for the door.

I ran to a corner near the entrance to the mall, pressed my hands against the sides of my head, closed my eyes, and slid down the wall. I sat curled in a fetal position, folded inward as if to protect myself from the massive emotional assault on my very being.

My body began heaving with sobs, and tears soaked my face. I began to cry out loud, quietly at first, then louder as I felt the dagger of grief plunging into my gut. I was wailing by then, but no one heard me because the clamor of the mall crowds buffered the sounds.

Sometime later, Nancy came to find me. She knelt down and put her hand on my head.

"Sue, are you okay?"

I couldn't speak. By then, I had stopped crying and just stared ahead, my eyes transfixed.

She left and a minute later came back with Edward right behind her. Together they pulled me up and draped my arms around their shoulders. They walked—or, rather, dragged—me to the car outside where Uncle Warren was waiting and lowered me into the backseat. They each climbed in on either side of me, and Edward held me tight as Uncle Warren drove us back to our hotel.

Nancy put me to bed, and I lay staring at the ceiling. Sleep came in fragments throughout the night, and the next morning, I found myself still staring at the ceiling. Uncle Warren came in and sat next to me on the bed.

"You have to join the living, Sue," he said with worry in his voice.

I still couldn't speak; words hung suspended in my throat. I felt disconnected from reality, like I was living inside someone else's dream. I couldn't begin to wrap my head around the idea that Joey was gone.

I eventually crawled out of bed and into the shower. Joey's commanding officer, Captain Bingham, was picking us up in an hour to go to Joey's unit on the base. We drove up to the entrance of the 47th EOD, and I stood in front of several non-descript buildings, one of which was a garage. Captain Bingham opened the door, and I felt a kick in my gut as I stood looking at Joey's blue Ford Ranger. The last time I had seen it was at the Kentucky reunion the previous year, and seeing it now was a cold reminder that he was no longer here.

We went inside the building that housed his unit, and I glanced around, taking in the sight of all the standard military accoutrements a military office would have: gray metal desk, gray metal mail bins, black desktop push-button telephone. I looked at the worn vinyl chair where Joey sat, and in my mind I pictured him there, talking with me on one of our regular phone calls of the last few months. I looked at Captain Bingham and asked, "Can you tell me how he got a Bronze Star?"

"He and his unit were outside Baghdad and came upon an Iraqi bunker," the Captain began. "He and another guy were the first to enter. They "secured" the inside and then started digging around for anything they might find. The bunker had been occupied by some high-ranking Iraqi officials, and some papers were found that Joe thought might be important. He and the other guy brought them out, called in a helicopter, placed them inside the chopper before it took off, and two days later the war ended."

My jaw fell open. Nancy, Edward, and I just looked at each other. For security reasons, the Captain couldn't say more, but I understood.

The second day in Killeen, I asked Captain Bingham to take me to Joey's apartment. I wanted to get a sense of his life as it was after the Gulf, to see his surroundings, how he lived. When I walked in, my nostrils stung from the odor of death still lingering in the air.

The living room was a mess. Magazines were strewn about, and an empty pistol cartridge lay tossed on the floor.

Whatever Joey had in his hand was dropped where he stood and forgotten. The kitchen table held unpaid bills and several opened handwritten letters that had been sent "To Any Soldier" while he was in the Gulf. A skillet that still had grease from a cooked burger sat on the stove, along with the spatula he probably used to turn it once or twice. Inside the refrigerator was a partially used container of milk and a six-pack of domestic beer. In the corner was a ten-gallon trash can overflowing with empty beer bottles.

This wasn't a home, I thought. It was a hideout. No art on the walls, no photos, no memorabilia or tchotchkes anywhere … nothing whatsoever to make this look like someone's home. The apartment had no life to it. All that was there were the scattered remnants of my brother's last few hours of his life on Earth.

I made arrangements for the funeral to be in New Jersey the following Monday. Joey's body would be shipped via commercial carrier, and his casualty officer took care of packing everything in his apartment and shipping it and his truck to my address. And I mean everything, even a used bar of soap from the shower.

I left the house early Monday morning, bypassed the church, and went straight to Norman Dean Funeral Home in Denville.

Tommy Dean made all the arrangements. His father, Norman, owned the small funeral home that handled most families' burials in town and had taken care of Mom, Dad, and Liz. Tommy's sister Sally was our babysitter when we were kids, and they knew our family well. Tommy had taken over much of the business, and he'd offered to pick me up at Newark Airport the previous night when I returned with Joey's body. As we drove from the terminal to the cargo hold (that's where "remains" are delivered off the plane), he turned to me.

"Even my dad can't believe this happened, Sue."

With no words to speak and little breath left, I fixed my gaze on the hood of the van as Tommy drove through the darkness toward the north terminal.

At the cargo hold, I watched as a large plywood box, about six feet long by four feet wide by three feet high, was unloaded off the truck that arrived from the gate. On one end of the box was stamped "HEAD." A hand reached into my belly, grabbed my organs, and twisted them.

I turned to Tommy. "Remember your promise, Tommy. You won't bury him until I can see him," I pleaded.

"You got it," he said.

The funeral home in Killeen that kept his body refused me that right for reasons I couldn't understand. After we had left Joey's apartment that night, I asked Captain Bingham to take me to the funeral home where his body was. I wanted to see him, in whatever state because I knew it would be the last time I ever laid eyes on him.

The Captain said nothing as we drove through the dark to the funeral home on the other side of town. It was late in the evening, and the place was clearly not open for business. I stood inside the door facing the director and issued my mandate: "I want to see my brother." The director and the Captain shot a look at each other. The director said no. I protested.

"His body hasn't been processed," he said.

"*I* am his next of kin!" I shouted. "*I* should be the one to decide what happens with it!"

He stood firm. I called Tommy Dean and asked him to intervene.

"Sue, I don't have authority there, but I promise you, your brother won't be buried until you are allowed to see him."

Since I was clearly losing this particular battle, I left, frustrated and angry, but knowing that Tommy would keep his promise.

Later that night at the hotel, I sat for hours in the dark on the floor near the window, staring out into the Texas night, feeling a mixture of closeness—Joey's apartment was down the street, and I could just drop in to see him—and at the same time, feeling a universe of separation between us.

He had slipped away in the night, and I got there too late.

But Tommy promised I could see Joey, and I trusted him. So when I arrived at Norman Dean's that Monday morning, Tommy was right there waiting for me. He gently took my arm and led me to a room in the back. Aside from a few chairs and flower stands near the walls, the room was vacant except for a casket that stood in the center. We slowly walked closer as the face of the body that lay in it came into view. The body of my kid brother lay motionless in his dress blues, which were adorned with the medals he earned during his time stateside and in the Persian Gulf the previous year. Among them were his Bronze Star ribbon and an Explosive Ordinance Disposal badge with its shield: a drop bomb, four lightning flashes, and wreath of laurel leaves with a silver star in the middle. A white fourragère was wrapped neatly around his right shoulder. On the right pocket flap was a small rectangular nameplate that read "LUDLUM." If not for this, I may not have readily recognized him. I hadn't seen him for more than a year, and his hairline had continued to recede. But more striking was the shape of his head. There appeared to be a ridge that circled from his right ear around the top of his head to the left ear. I turned to Tommy, who stood to my left.

My voice broke as I asked, "Where is the bullet hole?"

Tommy looked at me. "He put the gun in his mouth."

Tommy excused himself to allow me time alone. I leaned into the casket and gently placed my hand on Joey's. He wore white gloves, but I could still feel the plastic-like stiffness of his hands inside of them. I began to whisper: "I'm not mad, Joe. I love you. I'll always love you. Maybe now you can finally have peace. The pain is over for you. You're with the others, you're with Dad. I love you, I love you. Please come back somehow if you can, please don't leave me alone."

The church was packed with people I hadn't seen since high school, many of them Joey's friends. Also present were my college professors, friends and parents of friends, and neighbors from our old neighborhood. I sat in the third pew from the front and kept my heavy wool coat wrapped around me like a blanket of protection from the stares of sympathy and disbelief from the people behind me. I had asked Tom, Joey's friend from Texas, to give the eulogy. He stood nervously at the pulpit and struggled through tears to try to describe Joey as the brave man he knew and loved to the people in the pews who remembered him only as an orphaned boy.

The procession of cars, led by a black hearse, drove the quarter mile to the cemetery. The November cold sank its teeth into my skin as the wind whipped through the air and the trees bowed in mourning and gunmetal gray clouds hung low in the sky. I sat in the front row at the gravesite, in full view of the open ground in front of me, flanked by Leala on one side and my mother's sister on the other. Everyone else stood nearby, motionless as statues save for their dancing coattails in the wind. I had chosen a graveside service with full military honors because, well, Joey deserved it. I watched the white-gloved soldiers lift the American flag off the casket. I watched them fold it with precision. I held out my arms as they presented it to me. And I brought it to my face, the heavy cloth soaking up my tears.

I had been given the choice of burying Joey with my other family members or at Arlington National Cemetery since he was still active duty at the time of his death. I chose to keep him nearby. He would not have wanted to be next to Mom, but he would have wanted to be close to Dad. And Liz? Well, I don't think he would have cared one way or another, since they had no relationship at all.

But having them all together would allow me to visit all of them in one place. It required a bit of maneuvering because when Liz died, Dad bought a second plot next to hers. When he and Mom died, their ashes were buried in that one. So the question now was where to put Joey. Tommy suggested moving the two urns to Liz's side, placing them on top of her casket, and that would make room for Joey's casket in the other plot. So that's what we did.

The military marker placed at the foot of Joey's grave gave the date of death as October 27. But that was the day he was found. I believe he died two days before, shortly after my last phone conversation with him that Friday evening. He didn't show up for a mandatory meeting with his unit the next morning, and Saturday's mail was still in his mailbox. More disturbing to me, the tenants in the apartment above his said they heard a sudden noise late that night that seemed to come from his apartment.

Friday was October 25, the same day little Mary Pamille died so many years before when my parents were still newlyweds.

The Heart Bleeds Still

You don't die from a broken heart. You die from cementing over the broken heart. The heart is meant to bleed.

—Nancy Slonim Aronie

Over the next several weeks, grief began to again carve a fissure deep into my soul. It cut into every organ, every breath, and every molecule. The pain bubbled up from a cauldron of anguish, and I didn't know which way was up. I developed a secret friendship with red wine, sometimes consuming it with the urgency of a newly detoxed drunk. I wasn't sure if it numbed me or sensitized me to the pain, but coming from a family of alcoholics, I was all too familiar with its use as a coping tool, and at the time, I just didn't care. I cried myself into exhaustion night after night. Alone in my bed, I'd sit staring into the darkness, talking to Joey, just like when Mom talked to Liz during her lonely nights upstairs in Liz's room. My eyes scanned the room for any sign of movement, believing he would come back to me, show me a sign, anything. But he never did. I sat alone, whispering into the emptiness of the room, feeling more abandoned as my whispers went unanswered.

I am completely alone now, I thought. The last of them is gone. I'm no longer anyone's daughter, anyone's sister. This must be what being an orphan feels like. There's no one who shares my history. A void surrounded me like I was floating in outer space—no air to breathe and no reference point for where my place was in the world.

What the hell do I do now?

I have to survive. I have to stay well. I have to finish raising Leala. Collapsing into another depression was a luxury I could no longer afford. After hitting bottom the previous year and fighting the custody battle that was still fresh in my memory, I knew that I had too much to lose if I fell apart again.

But I knew I also had to grieve, and I had to give my grief words. I had to stop running from it. When Liz died, I was angry at her and used my anger as justification for not feeling the sadness. When Mom died, I got through it by acting out. I started smoking, drove recklessly, and slept around. By the time Dad died, I had become numb. I did what I knew to do best, and that was to run away. So when the grief began pouring out for Joey, it poured out for the rest of them. I cried for the life Liz would never have. I cried for my mother's broken heart over her two lost children. I cried for my father's loneliness when we had cast him aside. I cried for Joey, the young boy whose father, mentor, and only real friend was taken from him. And I cried for me, for the incomprehensible and shattering sense of feeling so alone. While I lived each day appearing as though nothing ever happened, inside I was broken. My body hurt. The skin on my face pulled south. I forgot to breathe.

And yet, I managed to buy a house. I got a job with decent pay and benefits. I bought groceries and cooked meals and cleaned the house on Saturday mornings. I took care of Leala. But the rest of the time, I lay curled up on the sofa. I felt the intense pain that held me hostage years before gripping my soul, this time making sure no amount of denial or running would keep it buried. Trying to live one day at a time was about as ridiculous a notion as swimming across the English Channel holding my breath. It was too overwhelming. My entire existence whittled down to living one minute at a time.

Breathe in. Breathe out. Breathe in. Breathe out. That's all I could do. I tried to be aware of my body lying on the sofa; I tried to tune into the sounds of the house, the television, the cars outside. I tried to do anything that would make me feel the slightest bit alive.

My frame of mind wasn't conducive to doing much of anything except pull myself out of bed in the morning. I was desperately treading water in the rising tide of grief, trying to live a normal life, to be present for Leala, but the void in my soul seemed to keep growing wider. And if the depression wasn't taking up enough internal real estate, fear and anger decided to come knocking on my door. I'm talking primal anger, the kind that kicks furniture over and throws things and screams out to no one.

Together, they set up camp and made it clear they were in no hurry to go anywhere.

I was losing control again, and this scared me to death.

What if I don't recover this time?

What if I lose custody?

What if I lose my job? My house?

What if?

I started to feel like I had a bull's-eye on my back. *Am I next?* I thought. If I had it in me, I would have laughed at the situation. After spending so many years wanting to die and then reclaiming my will to live, I was afraid that God would now take me too.

Then an interesting thing happened. On one of those rare days when I ventured into town, I was browsing through a shop and came across a rack of puppets. Among the Cookie Monsters and Pinocchios and clowns was a furry white unicorn with a purple horn and round black eyes that seemed to be staring right at me.

I slid him onto my hand like a well-worn glove, and he seemed at home there, a perfect fit for both of us. I bought him and took him home. I named him Pokey.

Pokey became my best friend. No, he became my savior. At night in the darkness of my bedroom, I lay awake and slipped him on my hand and allowed the tears to pour out as I told him all about my broken heart. A faithful listener he was, bearing witness to my heartache and despair. I know it was me controlling his movements, but it seemed like he would naturally nudge up against my cheek and snuggle his nose into my neck. I cried and wailed as he gazed at me with those dark round eyes. He didn't question or recoil in fear at the scary things that came out of me. I could scream out my pain and pull him toward me, and somehow it would make it better. I eventually fell asleep, exhausted, with Pokey resting on my pillow next to me. When the days got bad, and the pain seemed crippling, I knew Pokey would be there for me at the end of the day. My little furry friend helped me to open the value and release the vapors of grief, allowing the agony to dissipate into the air and making it slightly easier to get out of bed the next morning.

I also began taking daily walks. I knew moving my body was important for my mental health, and for the most part, I had been able to maintain a running practice during my early years of depression. So I mapped out a route that wound around my streets into an adjoining neighborhood, up and down hills, paying attention to how my body was moving and feeling the rhythm of my arms and legs propelling me forward until I ended back in my little cluster of small houses with chain-linked fences.

I even met a man. Rob was from my old neighborhood and he was clearly interested, but I initially hadn't been responsive to his overtures. One night he called, and after a few minutes of friendly conversation, he invited me to dinner.

"Just dinner, nothing more," he said. I forced myself to go because it seemed better than staying at home, staring at darkness floating in through the windows.

He took me to an Italian restaurant, and he seemed to be the perfect gentleman, pulling my chair out for me, handing me a menu. I did my best to be engaging, but my heart wasn't in it. Later at my house, he sat down on the sofa and gestured for me to join him. I stayed where I was in the chair on the other side of the room, wrapped up in my self-protective posture of arms and legs crossed tightly. I stared at the floor.

"You look so sad," he commented.

"I am sad," was all I could say. I didn't want to explain to him that that day was the one-year anniversary of my brother's death. My sadness was my own and not to be shared with a man I hardly knew. I asked him to leave.

He called a few days later and invited me to see *Les Miserables* on Broadway. He knew I loved the theater, and in spite of still feeling reluctant, I went. Afterward, we battled the bitter New York cold and wind and walked—or, rather, ran—to Rockefeller Plaza to see the Christmas tree. I could see that he was trying hard to win my affection, and I did feel myself warming up to him, so after that, we began seeing each other on a regular basis. I thought that having a boyfriend might be a good distraction and possibly even help me feel better. After several months, it was clear Rob would not last. We both were high maintenance—him with his demands and insecurities, and me with my array of moods that fluctuated between sadness and anger, along with a ferocious need to be independent.

I went to Rob's house one afternoon to try to settle an argument he had with a friend of mine.

"You need to decide," he said. "It's either her or me."

I looked at him and said, "You're right. I've made my decision." And I walked out the door.

The last thing I needed was a relationship that required so much energy.

I also found another therapist. Considering my track record with them, this was no easy task. This time I was desperate to not fall apart. I had attended a service at the local Unitarian Church a few weeks before and was in so much pain that I spent the hour crying in the bathroom. Not wanting anyone in the congregation to see my swollen face and bloodshot eyes, I slipped out early and grabbed a bulletin on my way out. On the back was a notice about a woman who had a therapy practice at the church in the evenings. I called her the next day.

Laura's genuine warmth disarmed me and helped me feel better about going back into the therapy room. I was also living on a tight budget with a child to feed and clothe, receiving no child support from Walter, so Laura offered to work with me on a sliding scale. We met every Thursday.

I came to our first meeting armed with an agenda. "I have to get healthy. I can't afford to come apart again. I have too much to lose."

This relationship was different than what I had with other therapists. Dr. Schultze was a good man who bent over backward to help me, but I was so wrapped up in my illness and convinced I would never be anything but a depressed, psychotic mess that I refused to consider otherwise and, therefore, refused his help. And during my hospital stays, I didn't believe the therapists who were assigned to me were truly invested in my welfare (but neither was I, for that matter). They probably were, but the nature of their role as a hospital employee dictated a certain standoffishness that didn't allow them to foster a deeper relationship with the patients in their charge. Once I was discharged, our relationships ended, and I was on my own to find another therapist.

Laura was patient with me. I initially gave a bullet-pointed version of my history: the deaths in my family, the crazy relationship with Dr. Styena, leaving Walter, and his kidnapping of Leala. I had repeated it so many times to so many doctors that my recitation was void of any expected emotional attachment, like I was telling someone else's story. I was again covering my feelings with a coat of armor. But when she asked questions—the ones that made me dig deep—I shut down. Feeling vulnerable was a risk I couldn't take. The only support I had at home was my eight-year-old daughter, and I would not and could not burden her with the ugliness that surfaced in my therapy sessions, should it rise up and consume me any more than it had already.

"I'd rather not talk," I said one evening, taking notice of the protective posture I had coiled back into as I had done so often in Dr. Styena's office.

"Can you draw it?" Laura asked.

I thought about it and said, "Sure, I think so." What first attracted me to Laura was that she was an art therapist, which I had never heard of before, and because the ink on my college fine art degree was still wet, I was glad to practice my craft. Besides, expressing what I was feeling through visual means felt safer than hearing myself talk about the pain.

I liked Laura right away because she made me an active participant in my own healing. My first homework assignment was to draw the house where I grew up, my family members, and anything else from that era. That night, I spread drawing paper out on my dining room floor and began to form the outline of my house, then the door, windows, and driveway. I sat back and stared at it as though I was standing in the street seeing my house materialize in front of me, and I began to cry. A wall erected itself between me and the paper, and I could go no further.

"This isn't going to work," I told Laura the following week. "I can't do it, I just can't."

So she suggested we just start chatting and see where it went. Light conversation, asking just the easy questions. We avoided any topic I couldn't handle until I felt safe enough to go near it. Over time, I was able to begin looking at the scarred places and talk about them, realizing that the pain I felt would not kill me. One nanometer at a time, over the course of several years, became the measurement of my progress. Laura was infinitely patient.

Through my sessions with her, I was able to have a better understanding of my depression. Before then, grief frightened me, so I ran from it. I never processed through the loss of the first three members of my family; I just buried my grief and kept running. But it appeared like a rising phoenix from deep within and took over my absolute existence. As much as I ran, it managed to follow me wherever I went. It followed me to California the first time in 1980 and then again in 1983. It followed me back to New Jersey the following year when Leala was born. It wasn't until I discovered it cohabitating with me in the house I bought the year following Joey's death that I came to the difficult conclusion that it wasn't ever going to go away on its own, and all my running was tiring me out.

Trust was a big issue, but I was able to trust Laura and she made me feel safe enough to take a closer look at myself. Therapy is anything but easy. It hurts; it kicks you in the gut; it reaches deep into the depths of your mind and pulls out thoughts, feelings, and memories you'd prefer never to think about, thank you very much. There was the question of early sexual abuse. I never had a conscious memory of anything happening, but between Liz and me, all the symptoms were there. She had an eating disorder; I was promiscuous. She was an alcoholic; I developed depression. We both went after older men. And the list goes on. (Not to mention a relative we nicknamed "Uncle Pervert").

We also explored my father's involuntary absent presence in my life and how that may have played out in some of the oft-regrettable decisions I made.

Laura helped to guide me through my grief, to help me understand why fear was such a dominant force in my life, to understand the rage and betrayal I felt in the aftermath of my relationship with Dr. Styena and why it was, at the very least, justifiable.

"You know, Sue," she offered, "even if memories never surface, what happened to you at the hands of Walter and Dr. Styena was horrific abuse in itself."

One evening she said, "I'd like to try a guided meditation with you."

I agreed to it, and she told me to close my eyes.

Laura began: "Can you see your house, the one where you grew up? Let's go up to the front door and open it."

She guided me into the living room, very slowly, taking in the surroundings. The color of the carpet, the furniture, the stone fireplace, continuing back into the kitchen, the dining room, and then up the half flight of stairs into the bedroom area. I was fine with this process until we came near one particular room. I couldn't go in. Nothing surfaced—no images, no memories. I was just stuck. The memory networks Laura was helping me tap into shut down at that moment, and it was impossible for me to continue. We ended the session and agreed to maybe continue it another time, but we never did.

And then there was medication. I'd had an on-again-off-again relationship with antidepressants during my years of hospitalizations but never managed to stick with them. Either the side effects of the older, more antiquated MAO inhibitors and tricyclics were too debilitating or I felt too hopeless to be a compliant patient. As soon as I started feeling better—or decided

I'd never get better—I'd stop taking them, oftentimes the result of which was another four-week stay in the locked unit. I knew this, yet still objected to taking them. My rebellion was fueled in part by the memory of the cocktail of drugs Dr. Styena fed me, as well as the myriad of antipsychotics, antidepressants, and anti-anxiety drugs I was required to take in the hospital. I wanted control over myself now, and the only way to have it was to refuse medication.

"They're just a placebo," I belligerently said to Dr. Schultze when I was still his patient. "I don't need them."

If anybody needed them, I surely did. But in my recalcitrance, he couldn't convince me of that. We'd had this conversation on numerous occasions, always after I had been home from the hospital for several months and again decided to stop taking the medication.

Dr. Schultze tried reasoning with me. "If you were a diabetic, you would take insulin, wouldn't you?" he asked.

"Of course. But I'm not a diabetic, and I DON'T need the pills!"

And like clockwork, it wouldn't be long before I found myself once again on the fourth floor of St. Clare's Hospital. It was soon after that Dr. Schultze decided he could no longer keep me as his patient, and he ended our relationship.

By the time I began my work with Laura, my attitude about medication had softened slightly because hindsight provided a clearer picture of my destructive thinking, and there was a lot more at stake now. I was willing to listen.

"It will help bring you to a level of functioning so you can start to do the work," Laura explained early on.

I also knew Walter was waiting for me to fall apart so he could take Leala again, and I could not let that happen. I reached out my hand and took the paper Laura gave me that had the name of a doctor who could prescribe.

Once I got beyond my reluctance, I became faithful in my adherence to the daily dose of Prozac, which was an SSRI, or supplemental serotonin reuptake inhibitor. I was fortunate to experience no side effects from this newer classification of drugs, and my health insurance covered most of the cost. The medication definitely was having a positive impact on my ability to function without making me loopy. It cleared the frost off the lens through which I saw the world, and I continued taking it for several years until I could eventually—and carefully—wean off of it.

In the meantime, my work with Laura continued. She offered me her hand to hold while I revisited some of the dark places in my mind and in my past, and she helped me understand the fallacy of my self-loathing so I could eventually forgive myself and even, dare I say, learn to tolerate myself.

Moving Onward

Screwing up is hardly a major mistake. Sometimes your wrong choices bring you to the right places.

—Shannon L. Alder

In the fall of 1994, I met a man who would become my second husband (my fourteen-year relationship with Walter was common-law). I was thirty-six and ready to again attempt a relationship with a man, and, truth be told, I wanted a family of my own. I wanted someone to love, someone who could fill the increasingly empty father role for Leala. Most of her own father's attention was given to his new girlfriend and her son, leaving little for Leala. I thought a man in the house could provide the well-rounded structural family that I wanted and she needed. And I also wanted another child. I longed for all the elements of a complete family, maybe so I could feel like I belonged somewhere.

… Maybe so I could feel like I wasn't an orphan.

… Maybe so I could feel like I had a place in the world.

I began my search for a viable candidate.

My friend Nancy and I attended a discussion about art at a local church one evening, which was followed by a social hour that provided an opportunity for attendees to meet each other. I had been cornered by a man with terrible breath and no sense of personal space who clearly was practicing his social skills, and I managed to excuse myself and slipped away to find Nancy. She was exchanging phone numbers with a man and introduced us briefly before we left. She later told me that she really wasn't interested in the guy she'd met and had told him as much when he called her, so would I be? I told her to give me his number and I might call him. I waited a couple of weeks before leaving a message on his phone. He called the next day, and we set up a dinner date.

Norman was a decent man, and at the time, he made me feel safe. He had all the signs of a potential partner—good job, solid family, seemingly strong morals, and emotional stability.

And with that, I entered into a relationship with him. It would be much later before I saw any of his issues surface, and by then I was already in love with him.

Initially, our courtship was wonderful and we rarely argued. Not because there weren't disagreements but because neither of us liked conflict and we both perfected the art of avoidance, ultimately to the detriment of our relationship. In hindsight, I can see that I chose to overlook things that normally would have been a show-stopper because I wanted so much to *for once* have a good relationship with a man.

Several months into our relationship, I thought I had become pregnant. Even though we were being careful, I was overjoyed and scared at the same time, and when I called Norman to tell him, all I heard were the words "problem" and "mistake." I naively thought he would share my excitement, ask me to marry him, and we would become a family. So I was taken aback at his reaction. A few evenings later at his apartment, I begged him to open his heart. He sat, staring at the television as though I wasn't in the room while I cried and cried, angry and anguished, feeling my heart breaking into pieces once again. He spoke not a word.

I could have let him go then and faced the task of raising a baby on my own because this was a baby I very much wanted. Without saying it, he made it clear that I had an ultimatum, and I was on my own with the decision. I considered what my options were: keep the baby and watch him walk away or give it up and hold onto the promise he made of a future with him, as he put it, "when I'm ready." I should have known then that if a man isn't ready by the time he's forty-six, he never will be. A week later, my period came. And I stayed with him.

Two years later, I called in the loan. Norman had promised me a future with him, and I was done waiting. I woke up one Saturday morning, him stirring next to me, and I decided to bring up the topic of marriage.

"I love you and want to marry you. What do you want?"

He said, "I'm terribly afraid of marriage, but I'm more afraid of losing you, so I guess we'll get married."

That was it. Marrying me was the less painful move.

"I feel sick," he said.

"I have a headache," I replied.

The ring was pretty and one that we chose together, but I couldn't be sure if I'd ever wear it because even though we had at that point been dating for close to three years, he still hadn't told his parents we were engaged. Was he ashamed? I knew his mother liked me because he wouldn't have stayed in the relationship if I didn't meet with her approval. Mother *always* comes first. But living in limbo, not knowing if I would be one of those forever-engaged women or actually someone's wife, didn't suit me. I told him that he had to let them in on this tiny little piece of news that their oldest son was actually, *finally*, leaving the nest at forty-eight years old.

The announcement to Norman's parents was made after a sleepless night (on his part) and was not the romantic one I had hoped for. We were with his parents at Easter brunch at a restaurant of Mother's choosing. We always went where Mother wanted to go, no questions asked. That was okay. But what wasn't all right was when he told me that he had been up all night, sick, trying to muster the courage to tell his parents. I cringed, squashing the sick feeling in the pit of my stomach.

So brunch was over, and Mother, Father, and I sat at our table with the dirty plates, empty coffee cups, and uncomfortable silence between us while Norman had been in the bathroom for half an hour. I wondered if he was dead on the floor, lurching over the toilet hurling his food, or had escaped out the back door. I was about to knock on the men's room door when he finally emerged and returned to his seat next to me. I didn't know what he had been doing, and I didn't want to know. What I did know was that if he couldn't man up at this moment, I was through with the relationship. I didn't want to marry someone who I was beginning to believe didn't want to marry me.

He took a deep breath and began. "Mother, Father, I have something to tell you." He was able to squeak out words to the effect that we were getting married, but it came out more like an apology than a declaration of love for me. The room started to spin.

"You know I'm very loyal to you, but …"

Spinning faster.

"I promise to move back here with you when I retire …"

I swear I was about to fall off my chair.

He finally stopped talking when I suppose he had nothing more to say and had convinced them—or himself—that this diversion from the family order was a temporary lapse in sanity on his part.

I then said, "This is the part where you take my hand and kiss me, honey." To which he placed his now sweaty hand on top of mine and leaned over so his lips quickly skimmed past mine. By then, *I* wanted to lurch over the toilet and hurl my food.

The rest of the day was a fog. My stomach clenched, my heart felt pierced, and the voice inside was screaming *"RUN! RUN!"* Maybe this was one time it would have been wise to listen.

Ohhh, the signs we ignore while trying to fulfill our agendas.

I told myself that once we were married, he would make his home with me. This was the normal course of events, after all, and I assumed we would settle in our own home together in New Jersey, where we both lived.

The wedding was outdoors at noon on a Sunday in September. Vivaldi's *Four Seasons* resonated from the Princeton String Quartet playing against a backdrop of a manicured green lawn that offered a view of a lake, waterfall, and a family of geese to complete the romance. When we began our procession to the altar, Norman turned to me and said, "Right now, I have absolutely no doubts about this."

I could not echo his sentiments. I did have doubts. BIG ones. But what can you do when your personal agenda has gotten you this far and you realize you're making a huge mistake? When your guests are standing, waiting for you to make that proverbial walk into marital bliss? So I walked, nausea and all.

During the reception, I danced with my friends. I talked with my relatives who flew in for the wedding. I ate at a table by myself. I looked around and saw that Norman was nowhere in sight. I found him around back and pulled him to the dance floor so we could have our first dance as a married couple. In the weeks and months that followed, when people commented to us about how beautiful it was, the best wedding they'd been to, the setting, the food, the music, I agreed, adding, "and I'm going to do it exactly the same way next time." No one could know at the time how serious I was.

We bought a small Cape Cod–style house on a quarter acre lot near a park in Boonton Township. One weekend I invited his parents for a visit with the hope of having a private conversation with Mother. I recognized that the unusually interdependent relationship between her and my new husband wouldn't change unless I asked for her help in letting go—even slightly—the tight hold she had on him.

"I really need for him to be here more often," I said to her in private (he was still making the two hundred–mile round-trip drive to her house most weekends, usually with a basket of his laundry for her to wash, fold, and iron). "I'm trying to build a marriage with him and can't do it unless he's here more."

She stared at me for a moment and said, "Well, I certainly think he should come home as often as he can." Meaning, when she wanted him to.

I clearly didn't have her support and knew then that I was in trouble. Building a partnership would be left to me and me alone, and at the time, I was still hopeful beyond reason that this would be possible.

Once, after a two-week period of Norman staying at our house, Mother called and asked when he was coming home.

"He *is* home," I told her.

"Well, you know what I mean," she said.

"Yes I do, and *you* know what *I* mean," was my rebuttal.

If she was going to continue gripping the reins, I was going to slice through them.

Six months after our wedding, I told him we needed counseling.

"I don't want to," he said. "It's expensive."

"Oh really?" I replied. "And you think divorce isn't? It's one or the other at this point. Your choice."

Our once-a-week couples' counseling lasted for two months and did little but fuel my anger at the situation. Our therapist's office became nothing more than a platform for me to vent my grievances at my husband's inability to embrace our new marriage and be the husband I had hoped for. For months, he couldn't bring himself to refer to me as his wife. Both the therapist and Norman sat, speechless and wide-eyed, as the walls absorbed my shouts and complaints week after week. Since anger had become my default emotion, I hadn't considered that it might be out of proportion; I felt it was completely justified. I was a lonely newlywed, and our marriage had fallen drastically short of my dreams.

Meeting the Inner Teacher

When the student is ready, the master appears.

—Author unknown

The sign read "River's Edge Yoga." I copied down the number and called to get information and arrived at the old building on Main Street in Boonton early the following Saturday. I was looking for something to fill my solitary weekends, and with a full schedule of classes to choose from, I'd have something to do while Norman spent weekends at his mother's. I also was curious to revisit yoga since briefly dabbling in it during my teenage years. The yoga studio was on the second floor of a commercial building in town and was the former rehearsal hall of a professional dance ensemble. It did look more like a dance studio, with hardwood floors that bore witness to years of pounding tap shoes and a mirror covering the long wall on the other side of the room. People slowly filtered in as I took a mat from the shelf and found a space toward the back of the room to unroll it.

Just as the saying goes, "When the student is ready, the teacher appears," I believe that when the yogi is ready, the mat appears. And I was more ready than I realized. Here I was in my first yoga class, surely confident that I could keep up with the other more seasoned-looking students. The years I spent as a runner and faithfully attending aerobic classes three times a week left me in good physical condition, but nothing prepared me for that ninety minutes on a Saturday morning stretching, breathing, balancing, flexing, holding, and sweating. I was so attached to my ego, or what yogis call *Asmita*, that I arrogantly thought I was above the challenge. The Universe had different plans.

The teacher, Ian, was a British ex-pat with white waist-length hair that he kept pulled into a ponytail. He talked about his time in India and referred to all the poses by their Sanskrit names, a language I had never heard spoken before. *Mandukasana, Virabhadrasana, Tadasana, Hanumanasana*. The words sounded almost poetic and flowed off his tongue like the notes of a love song skipping along a musical staff. I didn't know what they meant, so I tried to follow the other students. I watched them fold over and gracefully place the palms of their hands on the floor in front of their feet. I, on the other hand, locked my knees, dropped over, and struggled to pull my fingertips to the floor, only to get them as far as my shins. In *Urdhva Mukha Svanasana* (Upward-Facing Dog), I glanced at the woman next to me, her spine beautifully curved down her back like a ski jump, while mine stayed as straight as a leg bone. The final moment of humiliation was in *Ustrasana* (Camel), when I needed two people to support my weight as I grunted and groaned and balanced on my shins in a failed attempt to reach back for my heels, getting nowhere near them.

Hope finally redeemed itself in *Vrksasana* (Tree Pose). We lined up along the wall, each one of us facing in the same direction, and shifted our weight to our right leg, lifted our left leg, bent our knee out to the side, and placed our foot on our right thigh. I stood on one leg, with my hands together in front of my sternum in *Anjali mudra* and my gaze dutifully locked on an object several feet ahead. In the midst of this experience, I found myself quietly poised, balancing on one leg, just like the other students. I felt a humbled sense of accomplishment and thought perhaps I did belong there after all.

Maybe I can do this, I thought.

When it was time for *Savasana*, or the deep relaxation period at the end of the class, I gratefully lowered my body onto the floor and surrendered it to gravity, muscles twitching and chest heaving to draw in what felt like my last available breath, until my entire being—body and mind—settled into a quiet state of calm. It was glorious.

When class was over, I rolled up my mat and placed it back on the shelf, told Ian I'd be back, and walked out into the cold January air, which felt even colder from the sweat evaporating off me.

Something's missing, I thought.

I sat in my car and tried to get a sense of what it was. I felt different. Then I realized … it was my *anger*. The undercurrent of toxic emotion that was my constant companion somehow wasn't with me at that moment. I didn't understand it, but I didn't try to. I felt a calmness that had, for a very long time, been absent from my life. I stayed there in my car parked on a hill next to the river, enjoying this wonderful sensation.

This was big. Really big. Because for so long, anger had been the relentless tide that knocked me off my feet, its undertow pulling me closer to an emotional blaze that, at times, exploded into primal rage. I'm talking about kicking furniture rage, pulling the house phone out of the wall rage, throwing plates rage, and collapsing in a heap of screams and tears rage.

The depression had finally lifted enough for me to function fairly well but had left in its wake a firestorm of fury. I was An Angry Woman. Uncontrollable rage was the one element that still remained from the fallout of the last eighteen years.

So this calm was a new experience. It was like the toxic environment inside me had suddenly begun to clear. I went back for another class two days later. And then again three days after that. I was hooked.

What I didn't understand at the time—and wouldn't learn for years—was what was happening in my brain. The neural pathways that had formed during my darkest years were a result of thought and behavioral patterns that had been repeated over time. In yoga they are called samskaras, like indentations in a well-traveled road. My anger had become a knee-jerk reaction that was reinforced each time I had an outburst. The time between trigger and tantrum passed in microseconds, too quick for me to register why I had become angry in the first place. I just knew I was because I saw the broken glass on the floor and felt white-hot blood rushing through my veins. That first yoga class gave me a glimpse into a dimension of peace I didn't know. Sure, my body felt the workout, but my mind—my entire sense of being—had been laid out on a cloud, floating in the warmth of sunlight.

As my yoga practice grew, so did my ability to feel compassion. I'll call this the Old Me and the New Me. The Old Me was the anger, the rage, the fury. The New Me felt calmer; I had a longer fuse and was more forgiving of others. I wasn't so quick to react to situations. The feelings were there, but my reaction time was more drawn out, opening up space for me to take a breath and allow them to diffuse. I began to see people not as potential threats but as fellow children of God who were navigating through their own struggles. I was even able to look at Norman with compassion, seeing him as the product of an overbearing mother who wouldn't allow him to grow up. I was learning to send out love instead of hate.

A year into my yoga practice, my panic attacks disappeared. Having been plagued with them since that first time in my middle school history class, I learned to avoid any situation that might trigger one. In high school, I'd create one-act plays instead of reading my report to the class. Somehow, stepping into a fictional character shielded me from the anxiety that was so often present. In college, I convinced my teachers to allow me to give a private showing of my art portfolio instead of presenting it to a room full of students. I chose jobs that didn't require speaking to groups. Any situation that required me to talk to a group of more than three people would trigger an attack.

They were also getting worse and happening with more frequency. I saw my future self as one of those people who was sequestered in the house, afraid to go anywhere. In addition to talk therapy, I also tried biofeedback and medication, sometimes popping pills like candy, all in a failed attempt to bring my anxiety under control. But a year after starting yoga I discovered the panic attacks were gone when the usual triggers came and went without the panic surfacing.

Whatever was happening to me was turning me into a true believer. *But a believer in what?* I didn't understand how yoga could have such an enormous impact on me. It was like magic. I wanted—and needed—to know more.

The real test came one Saturday a few months later when I came home from class in what had become my regular state of post-yoga bliss. The New Me walked into the house to find Norman still there. We hadn't been talking to each other because of one of our regular arguments, and typically I would have ignored him and gone about the weekend by myself. But this time I decided to try a new approach.

"Let's start over," I said. "It's a beautiful day … we can just forget why we're angry and enjoy the weekend together." I hoped offering an olive branch would be a step toward fostering unity in our persistently fractured relationship.

Rather than offering the response I had hoped for, Norman reminded me of why he was miserable and offered a list of reasons why it was my fault. *He could really use yoga*, I thought. I still spent the remainder of the weekend alone, but I didn't allow his comments to fuel my anger. Instead, I sent mental images of loving kindness to wash over him, which helped *me* stay calm. Even so, I was beginning to see our relationship more as a situation than a marriage.

One night something happened that forever changed my loneliness. About a year into our marriage, Norman left to go to his mother's for the weekend, and I was alone again. I now find it interesting how my entire family left me and I ended up marrying a man who would constantly leave me. I wanted him to stay home with me on weekends so we could work on our struggling marriage, but his obligation to his mother overrode any desire or ability he had to be a husband.

He also didn't want to be around Leala. When she was much younger and I was sick so much of the time, often away behind locked hospital doors, she was a quiet kid. She didn't cause trouble or act out, and she was a dependable child. Now that I was healthy and she was a teenager, her growing independence, surging hormones, and unleashed anger added to the havoc in the house. Norman didn't know how to deal with teenagers and wasn't interested in learning how, so he left us both whenever he could. The traits Norman had that I first took to be stability and groundedness, I now saw as rigidity and one-sided thinking. He saw things as one way and one way only, and his refusal (or inability) to consider another viewpoint fueled my resentment.

So there I was again by myself yet another weekend, lonely, wishing for the kind of marriage I had yet to realize would never happen. My friend Paul gave me his ticket to the Richie Havens concert in town that night, and I decided that good music enjoyed alone is better than the company of an empty house.

I often went to the cemetery late at night—the gates always seemed to be open—and knelt in front of the tombstone that had all four names carved into it. I was glad they were all there in one place; it gave me the sense that they were near me. I'd been going there a lot lately. I needed strength, and leaning on the ghosts of my parents and siblings somehow helped. Funny, I knew I was sitting on top of bodies and ashes, but being there near the essence of them comforted me far more than did the arms of my emotionally (and often physically) absent husband. I spoke softly to them, asking for guidance, for strength, for them to show me, if they could, what I needed to do and what I needed to learn from all of the apparent mistakes I was making. Of course, it was always silent except for the cars driving by in the distance, but I still looked into the darkness of the night and wished them—any one of them—to materialize. I looked for a sign, the rustling of trees, a sound, an ethereal form off in the grass somewhere. Anything.

Nothing. The quiet remained. The stillness of the night told me to go home. So as I always did, I crawled on my knees closer to the tombstone, I let my fingers run across the chiseled stone where each of their names is carved, I whispered "I love you" to each one of them, and then I left.

However, this night I didn't visit the grave. It was Saturday night, Leala was spending it with a friend, and a musician was in town, which offered a nice distraction from my loneliness. I ran into my friend Annie and her boyfriend at the concert hall, and we sat together as I tried to focus on Richie and his tunes. I pasted a smile on my face so my sadness didn't show and no questions were asked. But they eventually were, and I managed to recite a well-rehearsed story for why I was by myself.

Later that night, the house was dark when I pulled into the driveway. No outside lights were turned on when I turned the headlights and engine off, so I carefully felt my way to the door. I turned the key and stepped inside into the kitchen, and my first instinct was to turn on the light. But I didn't. I heard something. My eyes adjusted to the darkness as I tried to tune into the sound. Something didn't make sense because the house had been quiet when I left hours ago. Music, it was music. It seemed far away but coming from somewhere inside the house. I stood frozen and tried to quiet my breath to hear better. I moved slowly into the living room to get a sense of where it was coming from. I was drawn to the stairs, as if something was summoning me. I looked up toward the second floor and noticed a faint blue hue of light spilling out from my upstairs office into the hallway. I climbed the steps quietly so whoever was there wouldn't hear me, or maybe so I wouldn't scare *them* away. The music became clearer then, and I could hear the words floating in the air: "*in the arms of the angel ...*"

I began to tremble as I reached the top of the stairs and had to hold onto the railing to steady my balance. I turned the corner and walked into my office. It was dark except for the glow of the computer screen and the green light that indicated the CD-ROM was running (it had not been on earlier when I left). I stood dead still in the room. My throat tightened as my heart pounded in my chest, and the nerve endings in my skin tingled from the energy in the room. It was then that I knew I was not alone, and I knew who was there.

The song I was hearing offered the words "*In the arms of the angel, may you find some comfort here.*"

"Joey, I know you're here," I said aloud. I needed him to know that I knew it was him and that I was not afraid. I'd heard once that if spirits can feel your fear, they'll go away. I didn't want him to go away.

"Thank you. Thank you," I said as I sank into the chair and stared into the dark. The music kept playing.

"Thank you for coming," I said again. I felt a strange calmness. Strange because I knew I was not alone in the room, and yet I was not frightened. I knew why he'd come. His presence was palpable, his message was clear: *I'm here, Sue. I'm here for you. You'll not be alone. Feel me with you.*

I did. I felt him in that room as surely as I felt the floor beneath my feet. This moment, this ethereal exchange between us, was what I had been waiting for. It's what I had wished for all those nights at the cemetery and all those years sitting at home in the dark. I remained still, staring into the darkness, wrapping my heart around him.

The song played out, and the room grew quiet once again. I remained motionless for several minutes, but eventually I slowly, almost mechanically, stood up, turned the computer off, and left the room.

I wandered blindly through the house. I was speechless, lightheaded, exhilarated, and maybe a tiny bit frightened all at the same time. It had been seven years since his death and at least twice that since the others'. Countless nights had come and gone where I sat in the darkness, summoning them by the force of sheer will. This night he came. He knew. In my loneliness he made his presence known. He *was* with me; they *all* were with me. This night I felt like someone's daughter, like someone's sister, like my family had never really left me after all.

This night proved to me what I wanted so desperately to believe all along. In my depths of grief, when I couldn't walk my path, when my legs had weakened and my breath was shallow, when I couldn't see even the moments ahead through the tears that flooded my eyes, I was reminded in the most glorious ways that I really was not alone, that the people I loved and needed and lost hadn't gone very far away after all.

God gave me what I needed and asked for—*begged* for—but only when I was truly ready to receive it. I was so angry for so long that God took my family away from me. That night, He gave them back.

Since I was a person who believed in signs (but so often chose to ignore them in the past), I paid attention to the one that came early in 2000 that told me my marriage was going to work. After two and a half years of enduring an unhappy relationship and three months into my forty-first year, I became pregnant. After all the praying, sitting in the cemetery at night, asking my family to please give me a sign as to what I should do, I saw my pregnancy as God's way of telling me that all would be well and that I should stay in my marriage.

Our daughter, Katie, was born in November. Six weeks before her birth, my husband's mother died suddenly. She was between errands one morning and walked into her house, not making it far before collapsing by the front door from a coronary. The mailman found her the next day. Although I was deeply saddened, I also secretly thought that Norman would finally now consider me—and our new child—his family (his father died the year after we were married). And when his job took us to Virginia three years later, I was sure that he would finally make his home with us there and leave the ghosts in Pennsylvania behind. Leala was twenty-two by then and, having matured enough to start building her own life, opted to say in New Jersey. I also said good-bye to Laura.

As it would be, the hold that Norman's mother had on him persisted long after she was in the ground. He continued spending many weekends in Pennsylvania, away from Katie and me, walking the halls of an empty house where his parents once lived. I felt both sympathy at his inability to break free of the emotional stranglehold his mother held on him and sadness over the increasingly splintered relationship I was a part of. My home was wherever I was living at the time; Norman's was an empty house two hundred miles away. I was building a home for us in Virginia; he was clinging to ghosts and memories far away. I was also getting used to being on the other end of his pointed finger, and it was bothering me less and less.

The following year, I met someone. I didn't plan it or expect it, but it happened. Norman and I were invited to a neighbor's Cinco de Mayo party one Saturday afternoon. He was ignoring me because I was guilty of some transgression or another—usually involving money—that I wasn't aware had been committed.

In New Jersey, I had held editorial positions in the medical publishing field, but the transfer to Virginia eliminated comparable job prospects. I kept my publishing connections and was able to score occasional freelance editing jobs, and I filled available time as a substitute teacher. I made up for my lack of financial contribution by taking on full responsibility for cooking, cleaning, laundry, shopping, painting, landscaping, completing house repairs, and being mom to our three-year-old daughter. Norman saw his income as his money, and since I brought in very little in the way of a paycheck, I had to ask him for enough each month to pay the bills, which usually triggered an argument and the comment "quit hassling me." He made enough to support two households but continued to live with the ingrained attitude that poverty was one electric bill away.

Back to Cinco de Mayo. We were at the party, with several people from the neighborhood inside, outside, on the deck, and in the yard. My daughter was playing with the other kids. Someone handed me a daiquiri and said, "It's Eric's secret recipe." Delicious? Not even close. More like orgasmic. A thick crimson-red sweet-with-a-bite-of-naughty concoction. Oooh, yeah. Deliciously cool. I sipped it down.

Moving from the deck to the kitchen to refill my glass, I saw him. He was standing in front of his blender of homemade orgasm juice when my friend Julianna said, "Sue, this is Eric." We shook hands, and at first, I thought nothing of it. Here was another good-looking guy with a sexy smile, dark Marine Corps–buzzed hair, buff upper body, and a killer rope tattoo wrapped around his well-defined bicep. I felt chatty, so I said, "Okay, give it up. What's in it?" He must have been a little transfixed because he started naming the ingredients. He later told me that until then, he had kept the recipe a secret.

We chatted a few more minutes, and then I wandered back out to the deck. While I leaned on the railing and was engaged in conversation with someone, I noticed him somewhere behind me. Actually, I noticed him noticing me. Playing it cool, I ignored him. After all, I was married and taking my vows seriously, even when it came to flirting. Even though I was miserable. Even though I was desperately lonely. Even though my heart was longing for someone to fill it. Even though my husband was ignoring me. Eric later told me he had no idea my husband was even at the party.

Sometimes seemingly big things happen even though you can't remember the details, and my big thing was getting Eric's phone number, a violation of personal morals. An affair was not my intention, but I was drawn to him and almost couldn't help myself. And I knew he was drawn to me. I was starving in my marriage. My husband was an emotional shell, and the only loyalty he truly had was to his mother, who he still clung to long after she was six feet under.

So a few days later, I called Eric. I made up a reason and dialed his number. I then found another reason to knock on his door. It's funny, the games we play even when we're adults. I'm sure he knew it was a ruse, but he didn't seem to mind. He loved the attention. My attraction toward him grew, and I found myself in an interesting place. I had been living in the darkness of an empty marriage with a man who probably never wanted to be married, and the lights were suddenly turned on. There were other men out there, men who paid attention to me, who laughed with passion, who were not afraid to cry, who loved life. Norman was one-dimensional, a Flat Stanley of sorts. In contrast, Eric was a full-spectrum, three-dimensional Adonis who reeked of aliveness. Eric was my sip of water in an otherwise arid desert.

He became the catalyst that led me to the decision to end my marriage. I had been lonely too long and wanted and needed to make my life more than a solitary journey of merely hanging on till death do us part because I was already dying. After getting away from Walter, I promised myself that no man would ever kill my spirit. Norman didn't intentionally try to do it, but his mother issues, his rigidity, and his judgmental disposition chipped away at me enough until I realized I had to leave.

Over the next several weeks, Eric and I became close, and I asked him if he would wait for me.

"I can't," he said. "I waited for someone for three years, but then she went back to her husband." I tried to tell him that I wouldn't do that and that my mind was made up. But he was unyielding. My heart sank, and out of a need for self-preservation, I closed it on him. I stopped visiting him, stopped all phone calls, and worked hard to stop thinking about him. I looked the other way when I passed his house so I wouldn't have to see other women's cars there. I was running again. Running away from both a failed marriage and the disappointment of a hoped-for relationship. I had to let them both go.

Eric wasn't the reason I left my husband, but he was the motivation I needed to make my first move. I was grateful in the end because our friendship and my attraction to him began a trajectory that would eventually liberate me and lead me in a direction where I would one day find real love.

The motivational speaker Anthony Robbins says no one changes until the pain of staying where you are becomes greater than making a change. My marriage was lonely, and my heart was breaking over the loss of an unfulfilled dream. I wanted a partnership and companionship but wasn't getting either. My daughter and I had been left alone long enough, and I was done. I was ready to make a change.

Norman's house in Pennsylvania was kept exactly as it was the day his mother died (down to her shopping list on the kitchen table). He allowed no one else to live there. He had always kept it as his legal residence. It was where he had his mail sent, where he kept his financial records, legal documents, and books. It was where he did his banking and shopping. It hurt to know that my husband— the man who was supposed to be my partner in life—kept most of his life separate from me. I had long ago stopped asking him to stay home with us because if he did, it would be out of reluctance; he'd be miserable, and I would somehow be the one to blame.

So the lesser of the two evils was to let him go off on his own and leave us at home. Truth be told, it afforded me time to plan my exit strategy.

Meanwhile, I decided to delve deeper into the study of yoga and signed up for a teacher training course, which was the only way I knew of to learn about yoga on a deeper level. Although I initially had no interest in teaching, I eventually did begin offering classes after receiving my initial certification (an accomplishment that would not have been possible if I was still having panic attacks). Feeling like there was so much more I needed to learn, I soon enrolled in an advanced training program.

As my teaching skills grew, so did my understanding of the foundation of philosophy on which yoga is built and how I could incorporate this philosophy into my life. I went to ashrams, attended retreats, and studied with teachers who were well versed in the field. I read books and research studies and sought out any credible source I could find to help me understand and integrate into my life this amazing practice. Most available yoga teachings have their roots in the Vedas, a collection of knowledge and wisdom that originated in ancient India and nearby regions thousands of years ago. I found that these same teachings are just as relevant in my life today as they were back then.

The message was simple, yet so profound: to live a just life, free from pain and suffering. And yoga is a path out of pain and suffering.

One of the texts that is central to a yoga teacher training is the *Yoga Sutras*. The root of the word "sutra" is "siv," which means "that which sews or holds things together" (think of the word *suture*). The *Yoga Sutras* are a collection of 195 aphorisms that guide the student toward a more pure and healthy way of living, free of afflictions, free of suffering.

Integral to the *Yoga Sutras* is Ashtanga, or the eight-fold path of yoga. These are tenets that build upon each other and serve as guideposts along the way to emotional and spiritual freedom. They are broken down into eight sections, the first two being Yamas and Niyamas. Yamas are restraints, or principles upon which we adhere to moral codes, whereas Niyamas are observances, or principles of living a healthy and pure life free of mental and emotional afflictions.

The first of the Yamas is *Ahimsa*, or non-violence. Without this, it would be impossible to achieve all the others that follow. It occurred to me that they were not only referring to physical or sexual violence but the kind of violence we commit on a more subtle level: our thoughts toward ourselves and others.

I realized that I was guilty of committing this violence through my anger and self-loathing. Because I had been filled with anger for so long, I had created a toxic environment within my body and my soul. I had to let it go before it completely ate away at my very being.

It's been said that hating someone is like drinking poison and expecting the other person to die. I was chugging it down, but the only person who was suffering was me. I also cast judgment after judgment upon myself for the thoughts I had about myself, which grew into full-blown belief systems that only exacerbated my depression.

Anger and hatred no longer had a place in my life, and with the help of the resources I found and my personal practice, I worked to make more room in my heart for love and compassion.

Learning to love myself was the hardest. I hated who I had been as a younger adult; I saw myself as selfish, uncaring, a veritable hedonist looking for self-gratification by any means I could find.

It took some time to understand that if I didn't love myself, I would never develop the capacity to love anyone else. When I began traveling in airplanes, I didn't understand why we were instructed to use the oxygen mask before giving it to a child. But then I began to understand why: if I don't take care of myself, I'm no good to anyone else. If I couldn't love myself, I couldn't build the capacity to love anyone else.

I also realized that if I continued to label the people I didn't like with the karma they had to grow beyond, I would never like anybody. So I turned the spotlight back onto myself and learned to observe my experience through another lens.

I was imprisoned in my mind, and the key that unlocked it was yoga.

Divorcing Norman was one of the most frightening things I ever did, but not because I was afraid of being without a partner. I've been alone before but was seldom lonely. I knew leaving him was the right thing for me, but I also knew that honesty wasn't his best virtue, and he would say just about anything to get his way.

Although I met him years after my family was gone and I had successfully recovered from depression, he said he'd use my past to take Katie away from me. And that terrified me.

Throughout our married years, one or both of us would declare that we were done trying, it wasn't working, and we were outta there, usually making that declaration in the heat of an argument. This time, though, I felt calm and confident in my decision. I broached the topic without anger.

"Sit down. We need to talk," I said one evening.

"I have decided I'm divorcing you. Neither of us is happy anymore, if we ever were. Let's try to make this as amicable as possible. I'm seeing an attorney tomorrow to see what we need to do."

When he realized I was serious this time, he asked for another chance.

"I'm not ready to throw in the towel," he said. (Really? Even after all those threats to do just that?)

I told him we could try for another six months to see if things improved. After that time went by, nothing changed.

What sealed our fate was the day I came back from the funeral of a friend's young son who died suddenly. I walked into the kitchen with tear-stained cheeks and saw Norman waiting for me, finger-jabbing the air and yelling about some insignificant matter that seemed all too significant to him at the time. Already trying to recover from the emotions of that morning, I quickly left the house, got into my car, and phoned my attorney.

Norman wouldn't move out, so I took up residence in our guest room and waited for the obligatory one-year period to pass before I could file for divorce. Seven months into our separation, I underwent surgery to stabilize three vertebrae in my neck. The night before the surgery, in a rare gesture of civility, he asked if he could do anything.

"Thank you," I said. "I appreciate that. You can be anywhere else but here when I get home." I stayed in the hospital for four days, and my friends drove me home on a rainy January night. When we arrived at my house, I was relieved to see that Norman was gone, but so were my keys to get in. He had locked me out. My friend's husband broke through the back door to get in.

During my recovery, I was restricted from driving, lifting any weight, or exerting myself physically. One evening two weeks after the surgery and a week after Norman returned, he walked into the kitchen with his checkbook in his hand. I rarely saw it because he kept it locked in a combination safe in his closet.

I told him that the mortgage payment was due soon and we needed to put funds into our bank account. He still controlled the bulk of the money, and I still had to approach him every month and ask for enough to pay bills and buy food. He began yelling at me that I was again "hassling" him. "Can't you just cut me some slack?" he demanded. Instead of engaging in an argument that would have been futile, I walked past him and into another room. As I turned to close the door, he came toward me, using bodily force to get in. I leaned hard against the door from my side and, in the process, felt a surging pain shoot through the back of my neck.

He finally backed off, and I went into the basement and called Leala to continue a conversation we had started earlier. I told her what happened, and she replied, "What? You have to call the police!"

"He didn't actually touch me," I told her. "I don't think it's a big deal."

But she insisted, so I called anyway. When the 911 dispatcher answered, I said, "I just want to let you know what happened here tonight. My husband and I had a brief altercation. He didn't physically touch me, but I just had spine surgery and injured my neck trying to keep him away from me."

She told me she was sending a sheriff to the house. I said it wasn't necessary, that there had been no physical contact. She said she would send him "just to have a talk" with my husband. When the sheriff arrived, he stood near the door with a wide stance, arms crossed, facing my husband, and said, "Why don't you be a man and find another place to stay tonight?" But Norman refused to leave, and the sheriff couldn't force him.

I had a sleepless night that night, thinking back to the summer when Leala was seven years old and her father had kept her from me. He had falsified a complaint to obtain a protective order against me, and I was terribly afraid Norman would try to do the same thing, so the next morning I drove to the police station, signed a sworn affidavit about what happened, and later that night, four deputies came to my door with a protective order. I guess if he wasn't man enough to leave on his own, he'd have a police escort to show him the door. When he was gone, I checked his safe and saw his gun was still there (I had figured out the combination). A few days later, his friend came to collect his toiletries and some clothes. When he left, I checked the safe again; the gun was gone.

My blood ran cold.

After Norman's mother died, he went into a tailspin and was prescribed an assortment of psychotropic medication, which he was still taking. I was now frightened because he was an emotionally unstable person and had been without his medication for several days and presumably was now in possession of a loaded weapon. I changed all the locks that night and searched the house whenever I came home, eventually installing a security system. At the hearing the following week, the judge ordered him to stay away for two years.

A year and a half later, it was over. I was on vacation when the call from my attorney's office came in early one morning.

"Congratulations," his administrative assistant said, "you are officially divorced."

I took a deep breath and felt a cloud of freedom fill me from deep in my core to the outermost reaches of my fingers and toes. I was finally free, liberated from a situation that I knew would eventually push me back into the abyss I'd worked so hard to climb out of years earlier. I had vowed during our marriage that I would never allow him to destroy my spirit, and now my spirit was free.

Finding Home

No matter how hard the past, you can always begin again.

—Buddha

I knew Charlie from the arts community in town. I was still creating my own art and holding exhibitions, and I also served as curator of a local gallery. I will always remember the first time I was introduced to him. Another gallery in town was hosting an exhibit where some of my paintings were being displayed, and one of the artists said, "Do you want to meet the person who bought one of your paintings?"

"Absolutely!" I replied, since I always like to meet the people who buy my art.

We walked to the other end of the gallery, and she said, "Sue, this is Charlie." I held out my hand to shake his, and he enthusiastically took my hand, his eyes penetrating mine, with a smile as wide and bright as a crescent moon. I was a bit bewildered by this man who appeared to be over-the-top happy to meet me.

We began running into each other at monthly gallery openings. Charlie was a breath of fresh air. Where my ex-husband was Eeyore, Charlie was Tigger. He was always happy, always smiling. And he was deeply spiritual, which was a nice complement to the philosophy I adopted from my yoga teachings. There was just one problem.

He was married.

While we kept a respectable distance as our friendship grew, I began to see something behind the sparkle he showed at our first meeting. There was a sadness buried somewhere behind the upbeat front he portrayed in public. Then one day he told me he was divorcing his wife.

He confessed that he had been miserable for years. I said nothing while he spoke but thought back to the few times I did see them together and recognized the imbalance in their partnership. His sadness continued to reveal itself during some of the more personal conversations we were beginning to have as he opened up about his struggles and his marriage that had come unraveled. I recognized the pain in his eyes, a pain so much like the kind I'd seen in the mirror during my married years. I knew that loneliness. I then did something I normally didn't do with anyone: I told him about my past. He didn't recoil. He didn't run. What he did do was hold me. I knew then that I could trust him with my life, and this gave me the patience to wait for him while he finished his legal affairs.

"Divorce," he once told me, "is a hostile renegotiation of a contract."

Once his contract was renegotiated, he was free to move on.

One morning my phone buzzed with a text message from him.

"Do you want to run away with me?" it said.

"Yes! Where?" I texted back.

"Anywhere you want."

I always loved the California coast, and Carmel was one of my favorite places, so we headed there. A quaint seaside village tucked between 17-Mile Drive to the north and Big Sur to the south, Carmel is sprinkled with art galleries, restaurants, and a laid-back attitude of I don't-have-to-be-nowhere-anytime-soon.

Charlie surprised me by booking first class seats on our cross-country flight and checking us into the Carmel Valley Ranch, an upscale resort nestled a few miles inland among wineries and organic food markets. I woke the first morning in a king size bed that wore a white billowy comforter that made me feel like I was floating among the clouds. The morning light outside the window had the familiar crispness of California air that I loved so much. A soft guitar was strumming through the speakers of the stereo, and a warm fire was burning in our bedroom fireplace. I could hear Charlie in the next room, and he soon pattered down the hall and slid next to me on the bed, offering me a hot mug of coffee.

"I want this week to be just about us," he said, smiling down at me. "No distractions, no work, just you and me spending time together."

And that's what we did.

Our first day, we bought lunch at a nearby organic market and went to the beach to eat. The wind was blowing the sand in our faces, so we leaned up against a fallen tree and swaddled ourselves in a blanket with our backs to the water. We could see the steeple of a nearby monastery and watched birds fly overhead.

"For years I've had dreams where I could fly," I whispered.

"My wish is that you will always have your wings, and I'll do whatever I can to help make that happen," Charlie whispered back.

That night, we drank the wine we bought at a local tasting room and made love in our bed, the glow of the fireplace being the only light in the room. We lay wrapped around each other afterward as my thoughts drifted to wondering how I ever got there, in that beautiful place with this beautiful man.

"Thank you, God," I said to myself.

The rest of the week, we kayaked in Monterey Bay and had dinner at a small beachside eatery in Carmel Village that served an abundance of raw oysters and ice-cold beer. We attended a yoga class (at my request). Charlie had never done yoga before, so I found a class that would be appropriate for a newbie. As we perched ourselves in *Adho Mukha Svanasana* (Downward-Facing Dog), I peeked over and saw Charlie struggling, his arms shaking to hold himself up. The teacher lovingly instructed him to plant his finger mounds firmly on the floor and engage his arm and core muscles, which seemed to ease the effort somewhat. He later told me he now had a new appreciation for people who do yoga; he had no idea it was so challenging.

Welcome to my journey, I laughed to myself.

We drove along the Pacific Coast Highway and picnicked at Pfeiffer Beach, where I fell asleep and woke up later to find Charlie holding a napkin in the air to shield my face from the sun. He saw my eyes open, and a smile spread across his face. Propped up on one elbow, he slowly leaned down and gently placed his lips on mine, lingering there for more than a few seconds.

Oh, how that man melted me. We made love again that night and for several nights after.

Our last morning, we sat in the living room having breakfast.

"I just want you to know that I have no doubts about us," Charlie offered.

He said that he knew what his feelings for me were but needed time away with me with no distractions in order to know for sure.

"I'm ready to move forward with our relationship," he added.

And so was I, but I had to consider Katie in the mix. She was still quite young, and it was important to me for both her and Charlie to embrace each other. When I was married to Katie's father, he barely tolerated Leala as she was growing up, and that just wasn't good enough for me this time. Charlie had to be all in.

I was a package deal. But he understood this, being a single father himself, and offered patience, love, and lots of humor to both Katie and me as their—and our—relationship grew.

And we had Charlie's teenage son, James, to consider as well. His ex-wife didn't want custody, and he needed to feel like he somehow belonged somewhere. Charlie often traveled for work, so James lived with Katie and me during those times. He had his own bedroom and a place at our table. I drove him to scout meetings and friends' houses on weekends. Wednesday nights were family night, and now that Leala had moved to Virginia as well, she and her boyfriend came over for dinner, after which we gathered around the table for a game of Uno or Monopoly.

The four of us—Charlie, me, Katie, and James—went on road trips to Michigan and Florida for holidays and family reunions. We functioned like a normal family on these trips with the exception of sleeping arrangements. Charlie and I agreed that since we were not married, we would not share a bed in front of our kids. Katie and James were confused enough over losing a parent, and we did not want to add to that confusion, so Katie and I shared a room while James and Charlie shared another. It just kept things clean.

One weekend in July, Charlie and I planned to go camping in Shenandoah National Park. Katie was staying with her father that weekend, and James was visiting friends, so our time was our own. I came home from teaching early in the afternoon to find a sundress laid out on my bed. A few minutes later, Charlie walked into the house with a map of Virginia wineries, which he spread out on the kitchen counter.

"I thought we'd hit a few on our way to the park. We could stop somewhere for dinner and get to Shenandoah in time for the stargazing lecture."

We packed our gear and drove west toward the Blue Ridge Mountains. After stopping at a couple of wineries, we headed out toward the mountains.

"Are we going to drive until we find a place to eat?" I asked. We were traveling further into the Piedmont region of the state, where the choice of restaurants was growing thin.

Charlie stared ahead at the road as he drove. "We have reservations."

"Of course you do!" I laughed. "You never leave anything to chance!"

We pulled off the main highway and ventured along a narrow country road, then turned into the gravel parking lot of a church.

I joked, "Yay! A church spaghetti dinner!"

"Yeah, well, only the best," he joked back.

He reached into the backseat and pulled out his suit jacket, which he then put on, and extended his hand to take mine. We walked across the street to an older-looking building with a second-story balcony and columns across the front. Two doormen stepped aside and opened the door, smiling at us as we walked past. We entered what was clearly a restaurant that was adorned with European interiors of bold draperies, detailed wallpaper, Flemish tapestries, and pink chandeliers with fringe hanging above each table. Clearly not a place I would expect to find in rural Virginia. As I was taking in my surroundings, a host announced: "The Booth party is here."

I spun my head around, and my eyes grew wide. I glanced at Charlie, and he seemed just as impressed.

We were led to a table toward the back that faced French doors leading outside to a courtyard. Our seating arrangement was side-by-side in a well-upholstered loveseat where we could look out onto the courtyard. The hostess handed our menus to us, which had that day's date and "Good Evening Booth Party" printed across the top.

"Seriously?" I said to Charlie in a hushed tone. "This is where you take someone for a special occasion! What are *we* doing here?"

"We're having a nice dinner, that's what we're doing," he replied. Charlie always treated me well, and he knew how I loved surprises. So this was one more act of generosity that he knew would surprise me and make me smile.

Our waiter, Chris, suggested the pairing menu, while John, our sommelier, began pouring the first round of wine into our glasses. I was on the verge of giddy but tried to maintain my composure as the staff treated us like royalty. Each course that was brought to our table was nothing short of a work of art. Orchids were tucked into sculpted glistening slices of fruit, miniature cilantro leaves perfectly perched atop a mound of cold-water fish that was just pulled from the Pacific Northwest, threads of julienne carrots and zucchini woven throughout peanut crusted soft shell crab tempura. And to top it off, chilled Maine lobster salad with marinated hearts of palm. On my way to the bathroom, I walked down a short hallway that displayed a wall of framed prints. One was a photo of Chef Patrick O'Connell shaking hands with the governor. Another was a framed letter personally signed by the Queen of England, thanking him for their lovely time having tea. Then there was the photo of Chef serving Julia Child on her ninetieth birthday.

This was a serious restaurant, and I felt like a young girl on her first day of finishing school.

We were waiting for dessert when three people marched toward our table in single file. The man in front was holding a round platter with a laced dome lid. Our waiter, Chris, was behind him, and our sommelier followed. When they arrived in front of our table, they turned toward us in unison. The man with the platter leaned over and placed the dish in front of me, lifted the lid, and revealed a rounded two-tiered plate covered in rose petals on the bottom tier and a large white orchid surrounded by white and pastel orchid petals on the top. Perched in the center of the orchid and hanging from its anther cap was a brilliant diamond ring.

I gasped as tears began streaming down my face. Chris pulled the table away, and Charlie knelt down in front of me, tears in his eyes, and said, "Sue, you're my love and my companion, and I want you to be my partner for life. Will you marry me?"

"Yes! Yes!" I laughed and cried and wrapped my arms around him. He slipped the ring on my finger and took his seat next to me as John placed two champagne flutes in front of us and filled them. We held tight to each other's hands and locked our gaze on each other, giggling and crying all at once. Chris then placed our desserts in front of us, and on Charlie's plate was the word "Congratulations" written in chocolate sauce across a ribbon of fondant. "Best Wishes" was written across mine.

Chef O'Connell invited us back to the kitchen to offer his personal congratulations. He ooohed and aaaahed over my ring and posed with us for a photo, and soon after, we left to continue to Shenandoah.

It was late when we drove through the entrance to the park, and we trampled in our dinner clothes through the darkness of the wooded night to where Charlie had surreptitiously set up our campsite the day before. We made love in our tent and fell asleep, arms and legs intertwined. I woke in the morning and held up my left hand, fingers spread, and gazed at the sparkling ring I now wore.

"We got engaged!" I exclaimed, partly to convince myself that it really did happen. I wanted to shout it to the world!

Charlie propped himself up on his elbow and looked down at me, smiling. "Yes, we did!" he beamed.

We were married one month later in a simple ceremony at a horse farm a few miles from home, then celebrated with close friends and both my daughters at a French restaurant in downtown Fredericksburg.

The man who had been my best friend, my lover, and my partner was now my husband.

Saved

To regret one's own experiences is to arrest one's own development.
To deny one's own experiences is to put a lie into the lips
of one's own life. It is no less than a denial of the soul.

—Oscar Wilde

The following summer we honeymooned in Hawaii. As we drove the Pali Highway on Oahu, I looked out toward the Ko'olau Mountains, their jagged vertical edges cascading down toward the sea. The afternoon sun cast long shadows across their surface, and in the distance, the blue Pacific swept eastward to the endless horizon. The realization of how blessed I had become, and how easily I could have missed all of this, filled my thoughts, and I said a prayer of thanks to God for not letting me take my own life so many years ago. I was fifty-two years old and finally had a life I thought was not possible.

I think of the things I would have never known—my beautiful daughter Katie, watching Leala grow into an amazing woman, my wonderful husband, Charlie, the friends I've made, the quality of life I've worked hard to build. And my precious yoga practice that helps keep me grounded and focused. I still fall from time to time, but not as deep or hard as I did years ago, and the recovery time is much quicker. I still experience the full spectrum of emotions, but it's a little easier to not let them hold me hostage because I have learned something called "being the Conscious Witness." This is a way of observing what's happening in my mind as though I am a witness to it, as opposed to having a direct experience of it. I can say to myself, "Thoughts are present," or "Fear is present," and it helps defuse the emotion attached to the thought. Through conscious witnessing, I am able to step aside and see my feelings as what they are—feelings. They don't define me. And they don't have to control me.

I am a soul who's been given center stage in this human experience, and I've been tossed about in the turbulent waves of grief, trauma, and loss. I've struggled—sometimes with what seemed like my last breath—with the war that was waging inside my head and have allowed my demons to hold dominion over me. I've tried hiding from them. I've tried running from them. I've given up so many times, only to stop myself at the last minute and take another breath. I've laid my soul upon the altar of Grace and said *I can't do this anymore … please help me.*

And I have ultimately surrendered, allowing the hand of God to reach down and save me from myself.

The Conscious Life

We can never obtain peace in the outer world
until we make peace with ourselves.

—Dalai Lama

Perhaps learning to meditate when I was sixteen was a subconscious way to tip the scale of the daily tension in my home toward a more balanced sense of being. I was a diligent practitioner, sitting down for twenty minutes twice daily to repeat my sacred mantram. It gave me something to focus on other than my parents' fighting, and it helped me a great deal while recovering from my accident, cultivating a sense of calm while my broken body lay in my hospital bed.

I had a recurring vision during many of my meditations. I was suspended in space, floating down a long dark tunnel that opened into a larger, darker space. Along with my floating body, there was an object I can't identify that was floating ahead of me, bouncing in slow motion off the sides of the tunnel. I wasn't following it, but rather, was traveling along with it. The tunnel was a vacuum of sorts, soundless as I journeyed through. I was curious about this vision, and each time I sat in meditation, I'd wonder if the tunnel would eventually open at the other end to reveal a bigger, brighter place.

It never did, and I never understood the deeper meaning of this vision; I settled on what I saw it for—a journey.

In hindsight, I see that vision as a metaphor of my life's journey. The tunnel was the twelve-year period of darkness, and the bright place I had hoped for is expressed as the life I now have.

I once had a professional astrology reading done. It revealed that I had been a warrior in a past life. I believe that with God's help, that warrior has manifested into this life and drawn its sword against the demons that haunted me for so long.

Today, when depression starts to surface, I try to look at it through a different lens, one that is continuously being cultivated during my time on the yoga mat. I've come to realize that what I've learned on my mat are lessons and wisdom I can apply off the mat as well. It isn't easy. In fact, it's constant work, but I know the tools are there for me, if I can remember to use them. Through conscious witnessing, I watch the depression, observing how it makes my body feel. I name it: heavy, dark, shallow. I watch the thoughts that are attached to these feelings. I tell myself that these are just stories my mind is telling me. I don't have to believe them.

But there are also times when I feel more weighed down by it, and all I can do is feel my feelings and let the tears fall. It hurts, and it sucks. But I try to not be frightened by what I'm feeling. I tell myself that it's okay to feel my feelings, bad as they may be at that moment, believing that I can ride these unsettled waves until I safely arrive on more solid shores. I remind myself that these feelings won't last. How long it will take, I don't know. Maybe it passes in an afternoon, maybe it takes a week. But I know it will pass. It always does.

I've come to understand that I may need to do this work for the rest of my life because no matter how good my life is or how happy I am, the depression seems to resurface from time to time. I do hope—and want to believe—that I never again have to endure that long season of dark night because my life's path has blessed me with wisdom and tools I can use to avoid spiraling into that scary place. I'm working on being okay with being perfectly imperfect. After all, we are all pilgrims.

One of my favorite spiritual teachers, Thich Nhat Hanh, says it's not necessary to sit in meditation in order to have a spiritual practice. We can engage in a spiritual practice in the way we approach ordinary activities such as walking, eating, and thinking.

I've learned that almost anything can be turned into a spiritual practice if I can slow down enough to really tune into the experience. Washing lettuce, eating a meal, walking along a path and listening to the crunching of autumn leaves beneath my feet, or sitting in a chair with my eyes closed and feeling the space around my body—it all brings me to the present moment, the here and now. I cried many times while writing this book. The process of writing my story has reopened some wounds, some of which had never really closed in the first place. But rather than run from the tears, I sat with them. I let them fall and felt the sadness purging from my heart. Crying became a spiritual practice.

I've learned to take a look at where my thoughts are when I'm feeling bad. Most of the time, I'm either occupied in the past—the realm of sadness and anger, or in the future—the realm of fear and anxiety. If I can redirect my mind and bring it into the present, those feelings lose their intensity.

"The mind is its own place, and in itself can make a heaven of hell, a hell of heaven," as John Milton said in *Paradise Lost*. But I am no longer a prisoner of my mind and I've left hell far behind.

In my work as a mind-body practitioner, in order for me to hold a safe space for my clients, I need to hold one for myself. I need to step out of ego and into awareness. But just because I'm still working through my grief doesn't mean I can't be present for the person who is sitting in front of me, needing to work through his or her grief. I've learned that there is a deep well of stillness and compassion that is always accessible.

I also need to pay homage to the field of psychotherapy and the value it has had in my life. I am forever grateful to the wonderful and compassionate therapists who helped me navigate through my darkness, who didn't give up on me even when I gave up on myself. I have been greatly helped by them; they were a lifeline when I was drowning in a vortex of despair.

The work of brilliant people throughout the past several decades has offered well-studied and extensively researched theories as to why people suffer. They have made valuable contributions to the field of mental health and have brought the treatment of mental illness out of the dark ages. One of the challenges of psychotherapy as it evolved throughout the early and mid-twentieth century is that the mind is simply too complex to draw a foregone conclusion about what's happening with it. Suzanne Segal said in her book *Collision with the Infinite: A Life Beyond the Personal Self* that "traditional psychotherapy is founded on principles that pathologize human experience across the board and measure success according to how well we conform to definite ideas about what our human experience should look like. We are taught that we must 'work through,' 'release,' 'deal with,' 'come to terms with,' or 'rid ourselves of' various aspects of our experience in order to live a satisfying life."

However, I believe what we're now seeing in contemporary psychotherapy has evolved beyond what was once considered the pathologizing of human experience. Although there is still great value in understanding the origins of our suffering, the processing and releasing of past experiences from our psyche can now be achieved through practices other than merely talking about them. In fact, the field of mindfulness-based therapy today is, in large part, founded on the idea of changing our relationship to our thoughts. The addition of somatic movement enables us to be in touch with our bodies and, specifically, the visceral sensations associated with emotional pain. It is then that we can begin to release them.

To me, suffering means living with grief, anger, and despair, and feeling like the pain will never end. I would never minimize anyone's suffering. My God, mine nearly killed me. But I now understand that all of these feelings—the entire spectrum of human emotions—are part of the human experience, and it is possible in many cases to live within these experiences and at the same time know that we won't perish from them. The DSM codes I was labeled with—301.83 and 296.34, to mention two— were merely numbers that identified me as having the illness they represented. They gave my illness a (sometimes false) name. I heard them so much that I began to believe that's who I was. Like a positive feedback loop, I became my diagnosis, and my diagnosis reinforced my illness.

Today I know that I'm not "Major Depressive Disorder." I am a human whose experience at the time was so painful that my suffering took over my ability to think, to feel, and even to function at the most basic level. That amount of pain caused a change in my brain chemistry, which in turn created a Conditioned Self, the voice of which shouted at me for years and prevented me from discovering a quieter voice—the voice of my True Self.

When I was recovering from my last period of depression during the two years after my brother died, I decided that I would smile at myself in the mirror each morning. I didn't know then that this simple act was also changing my brain chemistry. When we smile, our brain releases feel-good chemicals, even if we don't feel good at the time. This paradigm shift can be a tide-turner in neurological functioning. Doing this on a regular basis, as I did each morning before leaving for work, created new and stronger neural pathways in my brain, which made a small but significant contribution in my climb out of the depression. I didn't feel good when I smiled at myself, but I believed that on some level it might make a slight difference. Years later, when I began my studies in neuroscience, I was ecstatic to learn that there is a scientific explanation that supported the validity of my silly little morning ritual.

I believe the workings of the human mind are too multifaceted for any one body of science to completely understand, but an enormous amount of progress is being made. The field of mental health will continue to be studied, far into the future beyond my lifetime. It will be dissected, turned upside down, and shaken until all possible theories tumble out onto the examining table. But right now, the field of contemplative practices is gaining a lot of attention from the established medical community. Already backed by vast amounts of research, yoga and other mindfulness practices— specifically somatic movement, meditation, breathwork, and self-observation—have many of the components that can enable people who suffer to navigate through their healing journey. I was years into my practice before I stumbled upon the science that supported what I intrinsically knew—that yoga and meditation are powerful practices that can create a paradigm shift in how we think, feel, and function in the world.

For instance, breathwork—that which is the link between the body and the mind—cured my twenty-eight-year struggle with panic attacks by activating my parasympathetic nervous response, or relaxation response. Practicing witness consciousness helped to regulate my emotional limbic brain. Observing my thoughts has helped me build resilience against their effects. And even though I was able to engage in the process of healing in large part through yoga, learning that science exists to support its claims lent an even larger amount of credibility to the field of contemplative practices and further validated my own experience.

Psychotherapy and medication were two components in the tripartite of my healing. Yoga was the other. It provided a path to being able to access a deep sense of Self that had been hidden beneath the fears, worries, and anger. It has given me the ability to live in the full spectrum of emotions and somehow be okay with it because I know that I am not the emotion I'm experiencing at the moment. I can say, "Anger is present," rather than "I'm angry," and that helps me to separate my Self from my emotion in order to maintain equanimity. Too often, people take their thoughts at face value, believing them and assuming they are real. I certainly did. I know I have a choice: to continue carrying anger or decide to carry gratitude. I choose gratitude.

Practicing mindfulness and observing my experience through the lens of the Conscious Witness allows me to separate who I really am from the stories my mind tells me that cause me to suffer. It's only when I believed the stories my thoughts told me about myself that I became a prisoner of them. And I did believe everything they told me because it's all I ever knew to do. I know now that my feelings are just feelings, my thoughts are just thoughts.

While my first exposure to therapy was with Freudian-trained psychoanalysts, I'm fortunate to have lived into an era where some of the more contemporary therapies have drawn their influence from Eastern traditions of mindfulness. According to Dr. Zindel Segal, one of the founders of mindfulness-based cognitive therapy, when it comes to depression, getting well is only half the problem. Staying well is the other half. I know from my own experience how depression kept creeping back into my life, sometimes being triggered by something as innocuous as a fight with my husband. Key to the foundation of mindfulness therapy (and mindfulness meditation) is its emphasis on observing negative beliefs instead of struggling against them. I watch my thoughts come, but then I watch them go, visualizing them passing like leaves on a river floating by.

International speaker Teal Swan says, "What you cannot see is that the universe is always carrying you toward your highest good, even if the road to your highest good takes you straight through the depths of hell."

And when you're going through hell, what do you do? You keep going. Just before I hit bottom, I was in what felt like the deepest pits of hell imaginable. At the time, no one in the world would have been able to convince me that I could find my way out. Maybe it was the warrior in me. Maybe it was my innate stubbornness to not be defeated, although I felt very defeated at the time.

Whatever it was, I managed to take another breath. And another. And then another. And I found that my heart was still beating and I was still breathing. I was still alive. The path of my survival has been woven into a tapestry of stories from my past.

Today I am not merely alive, but *thriving*. I know I have come forth out of the gauntlet because the value of the life I have today can only be measured against the backdrop of the depths of suffering I experienced.

I now have what was once beyond wishable.

What makes someone survive? I believe we need to know that we do have the power to heal ourselves in many ways; we only need to learn what the tools are and that they are available to us. We do this in part by engaging in mindful practices like meditation to cultivate present-moment awareness, getting us out of our heads and away from the stories our minds tell us, as well as somatic movement to get us back into our bodies.

There's a term from Buddhist philosophy called *Sangha*. Roughly translated, it means community. I believe this is also an important component of the healing process. When I was depressed, I wanted to be alone. But this was the worst thing to do because it made me feel even more isolated. I was left in the company of my thoughts, my demons, and my pain that kept growing. Now, if I feel depression coming on, I know to pick up the phone and make a lunch date to place myself in the company of another human. I walk in my neighborhood and talk to the people I pass along the way. Interacting with people is different than merely being in the company of others. It's *engaging* with others; it's the social interaction that provides the healing component. I used to walk the streets of Manhattan, passing literally hundreds of people and yet felt completely isolated. If I would have stopped to talk to just one person, that may have lifted the veil of isolation and brought me out of my head.

I've also developed community of another sort, and that is my relationship with God. When I lost my family, I hated God. And as my life kept getting worse, I came to fear Him as well, thinking that I was somehow the target of His wrath. But now I see His presence in my life from a different perspective. The well-known poem *Footprints in the Sand* says it perfectly: when the Lord promised to walk with the man always, and in his saddest and most troublesome times, there was only one set of footprints in the sand. And the Lord said, "It was then that I carried you."

Perhaps God carried me. I believe the hand of God *did* reach down and save me when I didn't have the strength to save myself. I can't explain why I didn't die when I wanted so desperately to end my life, but I do believe the life force that saved me was something far bigger than my own. Today my community is my family, my friends, my yoga community, and my personal relationship with God, to whom I give thanks and gratitude each day.

For anyone who hasn't felt the poison of depression infiltrating their soul, it's hard to imagine what it feels like. Depression changes everything about you, physically, mentally, and emotionally. It literally hurts. Some neurons stop firing while others decide to take a different route. Making simple decisions becomes inexplicably difficult. Rational thought processes cease. We become a prisoner of our mind, and the stories our mind feeds us give us a false perception of reality. If I'm really paying attention, I can recognize that false reality and identify it as being such. I'm then able to pull up a chair and sit next to it, where I can witness what's happening without being consumed by it.

Does it take work? Of course. Is it something that comes easy? No.

That's why it's called mindful practice and not mindful perfect.

Hope

*Take a moment and sit with yourself. You
may find what you are looking for.*

—Steven Cuoco

When I was a child, my favorite movie was *The Wizard of Oz*. It
came on TV once a year, and I always looked forward to sitting
in front the family RCA television, watching in amazement as the
tornado swept Dorothy's house away, spinning it up, up, up and
seeing it crash land in technicolor glory somewhere on the other
side of the rainbow. In my young naiveté, I thought that part of
the movie was filmed in black and white because the studio didn't
have enough money to shoot the entire film in color.

I was too young at the time to understand the underlying
message L. Frank Baum was trying to convey through his beloved
forest characters, but as I grew and continued to watch the movie
every year, I could see a deeper meaning. The Tin Man, the
Scarecrow, and the Lion all joined Dorothy on her quest to Oz in
hopes that the Wizard might give them what they believed was
missing in their lives—a heart, a brain, courage, and for Dorothy,
a way back home. But during their sojourn, it was Scarecrow
who came up with the best ideas, Lion who exhibited bravery
beyond compare, and Tin Man's tears that kept rusting his joints.
It was an *aha* moment for me when I finally realized that they

always had what they sought; they only needed validation from the Wizard.

And Dorothy? She spent most of the movie trying to return to the very place from which she'd run away. She ran because she believed there was something better on the other side of the rainbow but realized that what she had been searching for was ultimately found in the very place she had left.

There is a stark parallel between this story and mine. I spent years running—either away from grief or toward the hope of happiness that I thought existed anywhere but where I was. I ran from my depression. I ran from my anger. I ran from my grief in hopes it wouldn't catch up with me. I ran to California because I believed it was the Promised Land. I ran back to New Jersey because I couldn't find what I was looking for out west. I ran into the arms of emotionally unavailable and sometimes dangerous men. And I was exhausted. I thought that if I could run away, I could keep away from the pain. It took a very long time to realize that all that running got me nowhere, that I had the strength all along to *sit with* my pain. It wasn't something I had to fight or conquer. It wouldn't kill me (although I believed at the time that it could). The feelings that live in me—sadness, grief, fear, joy, happiness, anxiety, anger, contentment—are all a part of who I am. But any and all of these feelings don't *define* who I am. I am much more.

The meditation practice I first began when I was sixteen came and went throughout my life. I would re-devote myself to it from time to time and then abandon it when life got busy or I became depressed. A few years ago, I took it up again and made an effort to make it an integral part of my regular yoga practice. When I again began sitting in meditation, spending time on my yoga mat, and meeting the Self within, I realized that what I thought I was running away from wasn't real, and what I had been running toward had been a part of me all along. Feelings are transient, but I am a never-changing spirit.

The sense of well-being I seek is within. The companion I seek is within. My true source of peace is deep within. I don't have to go looking for it in false prophets or selfish psychiatrists or the bottom of a wine bottle or a group of people in the hills of California.

The place in the world I had been searching for was ultimately found in the quiet of my own mind.

When we deny our right to experience our emotions, we deny our very humanity. When we squash the anger, or worse, act out in explosive ways, we are being held hostage by it. John Welwood says in his book, *Toward a Psychology of Awakening*, "The root of psychological problems stems from our difficulty letting our experience be as it is. Instead, we judge, react, and turn away from our experiences that cause anxiety/depression/pain."

We tend to interpret the world through the lens of our experience, which potentially reduces what is really a multifaceted, multidimensional, full-spectrum world of good, bad, and everything in between into shades of black and white.

I can also look back at the dynamics of my family of origin and better understand, to a degree, what caused them to act the way they did.

There's a poster in the stairwell of the Kripalu Center for Yoga & Health in Stockbridge, Massachusetts, that reads something like this: "Be kind to those you meet, for everyone is walking a difficult path." This helps me to see my mother through the lens of compassion rather than resentment. Did she damage her children? Yes. Did she love us? Of course. But she couldn't reconcile her unhappiness, have a place for it, and continue being a decent mother. I can now see that while, on one level, we may have been valued members of a family, we were also puppets, the strings of our hearts manipulated by a woman whose strongest ammunition was knowing that her pre-adolescent daughters needed her love and would do anything for it. I don't believe her actions were premeditated. I believe she was desperately unhappy, hated my father for reasons that I never understood, and didn't consider the devastating lifelong impact her behavior would have on her children. I've speculated that the loss of her first child may have developed into untreated postpartum depression that became stronger with the subsequent births of the rest of us. But I'll never definitively know. In the Venn diagram of my mother's complexity, her hatred for my father and love for us overlapped, and we were subjected to the fallout. I want to believe that if she had foreseen how her actions would affect her children long after they were grown, she would have made different choices. Ultimately, her unhappiness and her alcohol caused her to leave us long before she died.

And I also believe that if her behavior had been different, I would also have made different choices in my own life. It's been decades since she died, and I find that I still have a love-hate relationship with her. I love my mother, but I hate what she did. That is a battle that wages on in the confines of my soul, and I know that continuing to forgive her will set me free. One thing I'm sure of: I am a good mother to my children. When I was still a teenager, I made a silent commitment to never drive a wedge between any husband and children I might have. At times it took all the fortitude I could muster to not do just that, but I think I've succeeded. Some family dynamics are carried on from one generation to the next, and some need to end. Living out my mother's life—and thus having my daughters live out mine—would not be my legacy.

As for my sister, years have been able to bake into my mind the image of a desperately lonely young girl who fell victim to her mother's need to find some amount of control over her own unhappy life. Aside from her brilliant mind, Liz was an ordinary girl. She liked Clark Gable and Neil Diamond and covered her bedroom walls with posters of both idols. She watched *Gone with the Wind* over and over again. She wanted to live in New York City. She wanted to have a career in fashion. She wanted to have a life of her own. I'm now able to see her not as the older sister with the venomous tongue who tortured me, but as a girl just like me who was caught in the crossfire of our parents' unhappy marriage. She couldn't control what was happening in her life, and maybe that's why she became anorexic—to gain mastery over the one thing she could control: her own body.

Unlike me, Liz was probably never strong enough to break away. I had always been the stronger one. I had the tantrums as a child. I did what I wanted as a teenager, the punishment for which never measured up to the thrill of the adventures I went seeking. When I decided to embark on a cross-country hitchhiking trip with my friend Ben, my mother's threats didn't stop me (my God, what was I *thinking?*) Liz always stayed close to home; I couldn't wait to get far away. Liz never defied Mom; I turned defiance into a sport. Her need to be a good girl was inversely proportionate to my need to be a rebel.

I struggled for a long time with the guilt over not allowing Liz to get close to me when she decided to become my friend, but hindsight allows me to believe that I disconnected out of self-preservation.

As the years provided more clarity, I now believe what saved my life is that I did get away.

Another difference between us was my expanding circle of friends, both male and female, which kept me engaged with the world. Liz, however, was lonely. Her intelligence was both her gift and her curse. At sixteen, she could devour books by the dozen and let theories, concepts, and ideas flow off her tongue in conversation, yet she seemed to be an outcast from her peers. While the other students at the private girls' school she attended had dates or sleepovers on Saturday nights, Liz stayed home, reading *Wuthering Heights* or secretly finishing off bottles of vodka that were stashed in her bedroom closet. She only ever had two men in her life, and one of them didn't stay around long enough to be considered a boyfriend. The morning after her date with him, I discovered one of my birth control pills missing. I had to explain to my older sister that they didn't work that way; you can't just take one pill on date night and expect to not get pregnant. In a way, I had become the older, more experienced sister. No wonder she spit venom at me.

While Liz and I were dancing at the end of my mother's puppet strings, Joey was running for shelter in the fold of my father's affection, getting the love he never felt from our mother. The lack of affection from Mom apparently began when he was an infant. I say "apparently" because I was told by an aunt that instead of holding him, Mom left him in his crib upstairs with a bottle propped in his mouth (is it just a coincidence that this is how her first baby died?). And when he was a young teenager, Mom chose not to take him with her when she left my father after Liz died. And when Dad took him to visit Mom during their brief period of separation, she ignored him when he walked in the door. The handful of times Joey ever mentioned her were usually after he was well into a six pack of beer, and that was years after she was gone.

"I knew Mom never loved me," he said to me one night. For the second time in our lives, I reached out and took his hand. But this time there was nothing I could say. He was right.

So Dad became his only real parent. They went on camping trips; they went trap shooting; they even shared the same name.

But I'm sure Joey still longed for his mother's love. When she died, putting her out of his mind must have been his way of burying her. And when he lost our dad, his best friend, only a few months later, his world spun out of control. He enlisted in the army after high school, which enabled him to maintain a fragile state of balance for nine years, but eventually, the Gulf War, his isolation, and his demons caught up with him.

I've come to learn that the self-destructiveness of a suicidal person is not revealing something about his present situation, but is telling about events long past.

We had all been crying for help, each in our own way, but nobody ever heard.

This I believe: If I stood on that proverbial ledge leading to death and was somehow able to step back again, I believe others can, too. If I was able to hold on just one more minute, take one more breath, stay alive for one more day, others can too. I've made it to the other side of darkness, and this place is a beautiful place. I had believed with every fiber of my being that my life would end in despair, either by my own hand or by literally willing myself to die. Maybe it's the warrior that stopped me; maybe it's the grace of God. Or maybe it's both.

I was lucky to survive, and I know I will never be in that terrible place again because of the life-saving resources I've acquired along the way.

I don't curse the life I had, and I don't wish for something different. I can now be grateful for this life and all that has happened because my experiences growing up and as a young adult have informed everything I do, from the way I parent my children to my work as a yoga therapist. I know what joy is because I also know what despair is. And I know the life I have today is one of abundance because I can measure it against everything I lost years ago.

The writer Andrew Solomon said, "You need to take the traumas and make them a part of who you've come to be ... to take the worst events of your life and fold them into a narrative of triumph."

My wish is that my story has become a narrative of hope.

Most names in this book have been changed either for convenience, clarity, or to protect the privacy of those who are innocent. The name of Dr. Styena has also been changed not to protect his privacy, but for the privacy of his family. "Styena" is a Sanskrit word that means "thief."

"The Uninvited"

It arrived early August
The call that year
That was suddenly heard
By a child so dear.
I waited each night
For a word or two
To hear what it's like
In that place so new.
She didn't come back,
A word ne'r spoken,
She was gone forever
Leaving all our hearts broken.
Soon another call came
Still passing me by.
The woman wanted to go,
No need to ask why.
And like overnight,
The man got his command.
He'd been standing in line
His hat in his hand.
"Don't go, Daddy, please,"
I heard the boy say,
"I'm not yet done growing.

I need you to stay."
It's not what we plan,
I tried to explain,
Though I couldn't breathe
Through the tears and the pain.
You stay with me,
Little brother of mine.
We'll take care of each other.
In time, we'll be fine.
We both tried our best
To make a new start,
But the weight of our grief
Made us both fall apart.
I, with my pills,
And him, with his booze,
We seemed to be living like
We had nothing to lose.
And one long, lonely night
In the beginning of fall,
I stood on the edge
And summoned that call
That had come times before
Always passing me by,
Now my river of tears
Had surely run dry.
The voice from above
The one they had heard,
Was calling to me
With a different word.
You cannot come yet,
There's a child there, you know,
She needs you right now,

You must help her grow.
And the boy needs you too.
He, too, is alone,
He needs to know someone
Can give him a home.
I took a step back.
Yes, I'll wait my turn.
Perhaps there are lessons
I still need to learn.
I'll do my best
To stand on my own
But please promise me
You won't leave me alone.
The child? She will grow.
The boy, not to be,
When it seems he is safe,
When I think we are free,
When I feel I can breathe
And that he'll be all right,
He makes that call
In his room late one night.
He opens the door
And invites himself in.
He just couldn't live.
He had to give in.
His pain was too great,
His sorrow ran deep,
He was done with his fight,
He just wanted to sleep.
Alone, I now kneel
With my head in my hands
And scream out my pain

To my God, "You're a SHAM!
You take all of THEM!
But you won't invite ME!
What the hell don't I get?
What the hell don't I see?
You've stolen my rock!
You've left me alone!
I have nothing left!
I've been stripped to the bone!"
"Hush, my sweet child,"
Came the voice from above.
"I'm not ready for you.
You have much to love.
Like the child that you have
And another one soon,
And a man who will love you
From here to the moon.
This is your calling
To make your love grow,
You'll live with abundance
From these new seeds you sow.
Your family? They are here.
They're safe with me now.
They want me to tell you
They're so proud of how
You've grown in these years
Of trial and strife.
You've earned your degree
From the hardship of life.
One day far from now,
I'll send you that call,
The one they had heard

Back when you were small.
Your life there on Earth
Will have blessed those you love.
You'll watch over them
From this place high above.
The family you once lost
Long ago will be able
To welcome you Home
To the feast at My Table."

—Suzanne Ludlum
written April 2013

About the Author

Suzanne lives along the shores of Lake Mooney in Fredericksburg, Virginia, with her husband and daughter. She is a yoga therapist and works with people who suffer from trauma and mental illness. She is also an artist, and has exhibited her work internationally with rave reviews. Suzanne is still a warrior who hopes she has finally conquered her demons for good this time.

CPSIA information can be obtained
at www.ICGtesting.com
Printed in the USA
FFHW02n1726280918
48594497-52549FF